Public Expenditures,
Taxes, and the
Distribution of Income

THE UNITED STATES, 1950, 1961, 1970

Institute for Research on Poverty
Monograph Series

Public Expenditures, Taxes, and the Distribution of Income

THE UNITED STATES, 1950, 1961, 1970

MORGAN REYNOLDS

Texas A & M University
College Station, Texas

EUGENE SMOLENSKY

University of Wisconsin
Madison, Wisconsin

ACADEMIC PRESS   New York   San Francisco   London

A Subsidiary of Harcourt Brace Jovanovich, Publishers

ACADEMIC PRESS, INC.
111 Fifth Avenue, New York, New York 10003

United Kingdom Edition published by
ACADEMIC PRESS, INC. (LONDON) LTD.
24/28 Oval Road, London NW1

Library of Congress Cataloging in Publication Data

Reynolds, Morgan.
    Public expenditures, taxes, and the distribution of income.

        (Institute for Research on Poverty monograph series)
        Bibliography: p.
        1.   Income distribution—United States.   2.   United States—Appropriations and expenditures.   3.   Taxation—United States.   I.   Smolensky, Eugene, joint author.
II.   Title.   III.   Series: Wisconsin.   University—Madison.   Institute for Research on Poverty.   Monograph series.
HC110.I5R49   339.2'1'0973   76-50402
ISBN 0—12—586550—3

PRINTED IN THE UNITED STATES OF AMERICA

Institute for Research on Poverty

The Institute for Research on Poverty is a national center for research established at the University of Wisconsin in 1966 by a grant from the Office of Economic Opportunity. Its primary objective is to foster basic, multidisciplinary research into the nature and causes of poverty and means to combat it.

In addition to increasing the basic knowledge from which policies aimed at the elimination of poverty can be shaped, the Institute strives to carry analysis beyond the formulation and testing of fundamental generalizations to the development and assessment of relevant policy alternatives.

The Institute endeavors to bring together scholars of the highest caliber whose primary research efforts are focused on the problem of poverty, the distribution of income, and the analysis and evaluation of social policy, offering staff members wide opportunity for interchange of ideas, maximum freedom for research into basic questions about poverty and social policy, and dissemination of their findings.

To SUZIE and NATALIE,
resident experts in the
distribution of welfare

Contents

List of Figures

List of Tables

Foreword

Since 1964, the elimination of poverty has been an explicit government objective. When a country has established a national objective, its citizens and leaders are understandably interested in knowing how much progress has been made toward its achievement. For many reasons, however, assessing our progress against poverty is not straightforward.

Assessing progress against poverty is difficult because the well-being of the poorest members of our society depends not only upon how poor they are in absolute terms, but also upon how much poorer they are than the average American. The well-being of the poor (and the nonpoor too) also depends upon not only their gross money incomes but upon the taxes they pay to the government and the benefits they receive from it. To the extent that poverty is a relative phenomenon, and to the extent that taxes are not assessed and government services are not distributed among our people in the same proportion as is money income, ascertaining the degree of progress against poverty requires that we know whether the poor's share has increased. In this book, Morgan Reynolds and Eugene Smolensky attempt to ascertain whether incomes minus taxes plus government services—what they call the post-fisc distribution of income—is distributed more equally in 1970 than in 1960 or in 1950. Do the poor get a bigger share in 1970 than they did in 1950?

As the authors point out, this is not a simple question to answer. First, accurate data on the distribution of all taxes and government services, by income class and for both years, is required. But the distributional effects of many taxes and government services is still a matter of such theoretical and empirical debate that even which data to collect is not a settled issue. Consequently, Reynolds and Smolensky employ a number of alternative assumptions about the incidence of various taxes and government services. One of the strengths of the book is their presentation of alternative assumptions and the data with which to test them, so that the reader can see how sensitive their conclusions are to these alternative assumptions.

One of the most striking findings of the book is that, on the one hand, the distribution of income before subtracting taxes or adding government benefits—the pre-fisc distribution—was substantially less equal in each year than the post-fisc distribution of income; but, on the other hand, the post-fisc distribution of income changed very little between 1950 and 1970, despite the large growth in taxes and government services during these years. Taxes and government expenditures thus appear to equalize the distribution of well-being in any given year, leading one to think that the substantial growth of taxes and government services would have produced a substantial reduction in post-fisc inequality over time. Reynolds and Smolensky do not, however, find a substantial reduction.

One possible interpretation is that the pre-fisc distribution of income has become more unequal over time. Just like Alice, the government has had to run faster (tax and spend more) to keep up. Alternatively, it is possible that increases in government taxes and services have led to increases in *measured* pre-fisc inequality. For example, increased Social Security benefits may have led the aged to work and earn less, and to be more able to maintain separate households (rather than living with their children). To the extent that this is the case, progress against poverty over time is underestimated whether the comparison is pre- or post-fisc inequality. An old person who is able to afford to maintain a separate household by virtue of higher Social Security payments is better off than he would be in their absence—but he is counted as worse off because, as a result of the higher Social Security benefits, he is a separate household with low income rather than part of his children's household.

To what extent the fisc is compensating for or causing greater measured pre-fisc inequality is an important question that will be addressed by the next round of research on inequality. If it did nothing else—and it does much more very well—the Reynolds–Smolensky volume would be an important contribution because it sets the stage for this next round of research.

IRWIN GARFINKEL
Director, Institute for Research on Poverty

Acknowledgments

The impetus for writing this book came from Robert Haveman, then director of the Institute for Research on Poverty. He offered us two justifications, both of which turned out to be correct. First, he argued that a scattered collection of articles in the public finance journals would be missed by many who would want to know about our findings. From the demand for preprints of this book, we already know this to be so. Second, he argued that if we started over and reappraised all that we had done, we would learn a great deal which would lead us to new measures, new findings, and different emphases. This also turned out to be true.

In addition to Bob Haveman, we are indebted to a great many others. William Pendleton of the Ford Foundation supported an earlier series of case studies on the distributive effects of particular public programs, which played a key part in leading us, to our surprise, to adopt an old discredited methodology. William Cowhig, through the RANN division of the National Science Foundation, provided the bulk of the financing of this study and was a warm friend of the project in every way. H.E.W., and especially Larry Orr, by the indirect funding of this work through the general funding of the Poverty Institute, and their concern and interest in our findings, also deserve thanks.

Many associated with the Institute provided ideas, data, and encouragement, among them Bob Lampman, Bob Haveman again, and Joe Pechman. We owe special thanks to Sheldon Danziger.

Karen Hester and Felicity Skidmore were superb editors. Phil Doncheck and Robert Dalrymple were extraordinarily conscientious and unflappable research assistants, and without their patient dedication to accuracy out to five decimal places, this study simply could not have been executed. For Gini Martens, secretary, gang foreman, conscience, fount of good will, and constant source of encouragement, there are not superlatives enough in the language. Our thanks to you all.

Public Expenditures,
Taxes, and the
Distribution of Income

THE UNITED STATES, 1950, 1961, 1970

1

Introduction

Is distribution a sufficiently important problem for serious study, and if so, why?
[M. Bronfenbrenner 1971, p. 1]

This book explores the response of measured income inequality over time to a more comprehensive than usual definition of income, one that includes the benefits and burdens of government expenditures and taxes at all levels. To accomplish this, we have estimated the size distribution of income for three years: 1950, 1961, and 1970.

Even though this is a book about one aspect of income distribution, we have not been able to decide whether the study of income inequality is an important research issue. Such agnosticism might appear strange since so many others are passionately interested in the nature of inequality and, more particularly, in the nature of income inequality. Perhaps our uncertainty reflects our citizenship: in the United States, political concern and conflict about distribution have never approached the importance (at least symbolic importance) that they have in much of Europe and in the underdeveloped world. Nonetheless, it has sporadically been an issue in U.S. politics, although taking the indigenous form of focusing on particular rather than overall income differences. As Robert Lampman (1973, p. 88) put it, "No political party has adopted a slogan of 'A .300 Gini ratio, or fight!'" Recent examples of disputes over particular differences include the structure and application of general wage and price controls, public utility pricing, the share of those middlemen in food processing, and "obscene" oil company profits.[1]

Perhaps these examples stretch the meaning of distributional issues because, like many disputes that are ostensibly distributional, they are noth-

[1] As another illustration, Opinion Research Corp. reported in June 1975 that a national sample of 1200 adults believed that the average manufacturer's after-tax profit is 33 percent of dollar sales, which is more than six times the actual amount. Also, for the first time in thirty years, a majority of the public believed that government should put a limit on corporate profits (*Wall Street Journal*, 19 June 1975, p. 1).

ing more than conflicts among interest groups. Trade unions, Social Security recipients, oil companies, and public officials use distributional arguments to advance a perceived, immediate self-interest rather than to promote some more general reform based upon moral principles.[2]

More basic concerns with the underlying income distribution, however, have motivated public debate and subsequently moved government in times past. Adoption of inheritance taxes and a progressive income tax were surely instances, and perhaps some support for public school systems has rested upon distributional grounds. The initial popularity of Operation Headstart is a recent example. Nevertheless, it is accurate to say that most debate and government behavior have not turned on whether income inequality would widen or narrow. Plausible reasons are not difficult to find. As Tobin (1970, pp. 263–64) says, it is fundamental that "our society . . . accepts and approves a large measure of inequality, even of inherited inequality. Americans commonly perceive differences of wealth and income as earned and regard the differential earnings of effort, skill, foresight, and enterprise as deserved. Even the prizes of sheer luck cause very little resentment. People are much more concerned with the legitimacy, legality, and fairness of large gains than with their sheer size." Perhaps acceptance continues because mobility within the distribution is high. Also, Americans are divided along many lines besides income and wealth, and they share a distrust of government and the restrictions massive redistribution would require. Rapid growth has also deflected attention from shares. However, at least two prominent students of distribution, Rivlin (1975) and Bronfenbrenner (1971), expect revived public concern over the distribution of income and wealth per se, although political predictions by economists are not notably accurate.

Perceptions of equality and inequality concern standards of "fairness" or "justice" and ultimately involve the consensual bonds of a community. If rewards are widely and/or deeply thought of as unfairly won, forces for change are set in motion. By this standard, the income distribution generated under current rules must not be widely thought of as unfair in the United States. But the continual discourse on inequality subjects this consensus to repeated review.

Public interest in and concern over government policy in distributive matters provides a rationale for scholars to study income distribution. In addition to a vague and diffuse interest among the general public, which poses no sharply defined questions, economists also furnish an audience for work on the distribution of income. The interest of these two groups provides the

[2] Ludwig von Mises (Lampman 1957, p. 262) said, "When the American wage earner refers to equality, he means that the dividends of the stockholders should be given to him. He does not suggest a curtailment of his own income for the benefit of those 95 percent of the earth's population whose income is less than his."

market rationale for research on the topic; the impetus is not provided by some abstract concern with the distribution of income which excites scientific curiosity. Our agnosticism about whether income distribution merits serious research investigation derives from the ad hoc and disparate character of this corner of economics rather than from doubts about whether it will attract readers. As Mincer (1970) says, in an understatement about the distribution of labor incomes, the field lacks conceptual unity.

An Incomplete Review

In this section, we review the literature on the size distribution of income with three objectives in mind. First, we wish to lay out the various objectives of other economists in studying income inequality, thereby documenting what we allege to be its disparate character and its lack of conceptual unity. Second, we wish to show that this book deals with only a small corner of a vast field which thereby permits us to finesse a large number of questions. Put the other way, however, the great variety of issues in the field suggests uses for the new data series which we have not exploited. Finally, we wish to justify the expenditure of resources on this book by showing that it contributes directly to long-standing concerns of economists as well as of the general public.

Economists have been interested in distribution from the beginning of economics as a separate discipline, although their interest varies over time and space, and from individual to individual.[3] It is relatively easy to cite economists who claim that distribution is of primary importance, from David Ricardo and other classical economists onward. It is not quite so easy to find statements by economists denigrating the importance of distribution, but there certainly are some. Harry Johnson (1973, pp. 55–56) furnishes an instance:

> These misinterpretations of the problem lead to an exaggerated and naive conception of the importance of, and urgent need to correct, inequality. . . . The essential point in this assertion is that observed inequality in income distribution is, to a large extent, a by-product of the modern economic system. . . . Efforts to prevent this outcome [observed inequalities of income], or to cancel it out by post facto income redistribution, run the serious risk of depriving the citizen of the benefits of freedom of choice and self-fulfillment and eventually requiring a reversion to a more authoritative, or totalitarian, structure of society and the state.

---

[3] Dare we say that there is considerable dispersion of opinion among economists about the importance of income distribution? For interesting and more complete surveys of opinion, see Lampman (1957) and Bronfenbrenner (1971, chap. 1). Note that the distribution of income by functional share receives no attention in this book.

Similar sentiments can be found among other prominent economists as divergent in theory as Galbraith (1958, p. 88) and Friedman (1962, chap. 10). The conservative view might be summarized as saying that statistical distribution of income is a by-product or artifact of the functioning of factor markets. As Hayek (Bronfenbrenner 1971, pp. 10–11) puts it, "nobody distributes income in a market order." Although these appear to be powerful arguments against an interest in income distribution of either a normative or a positive kind, they either have gone unheeded or have been found wanting in one respect or another because interest remains nearly ubiquitous.

It is not easy to create neat categories for economic work on the size distribution of income, because the work is so heterogeneous. However, to impose some order, we choose to group into two general classes: positive and normative. The former is often defined as the study of what is, and the latter as the study of what ought to be. Although some grow tired of this distinction and others deny its existence, claiming that economics is entirely normative, the distinction is especially informative in the field of income distribution. This does not mean that classifying particular works into one box or the other will always command universal agreement. Some work contains both positive and normative elements. Somewhat ambiguous classifications can also occur because income distribution seems inextricably bound up with policy, even in the most scientific inquiry, because normative concerns appear to motivate many of the writers. At the very least, normative prescriptions to "improve" the distribution of income must rest upon positive knowledge of how the distribution is generated, which complicates our classification scheme. As a prominent advocate of the distinction between normative and positive, Milton Friedman (1953b, p. 5), would have it:

> Normative economics and the art of economics, on the other hand, cannot be independent of positive economics. Any policy conclusion necessarily rests upon a prediction about the consequences of doing one thing rather than another, a prediction that must be based—implicitly or explicitly—on positive economics.

Works dominated by a search for positive knowledge can be further grouped into two sets: those which proceed from deductive economic theory and individual maximization and those which are basically statistical or econometric in conception. Similarly, it is convenient to group the normative work into two categories distinguished by the motives that led economists to their ethical concern: poverty and inequality.[4] The poverty

---

[4] Pen describes twenty-one popular norms of distributional equity, cited in Bronfenbrenner (1973). Obviously, we have been parsimonious in our categories.

interest captures the concern with the material standard of living for people in the lower tail rather than with the distribution as a whole. The level of income of the poor is generally compared with some definition of a minimum level of market purchasing power. Interest in inequality, by contrast, could be termed egalitarianism because many people identify a trend toward reduced dispersion with "equity." In fact, distributions with lower measured dispersion are often casually called more equitable than other distributions, despite the numerous and dubious ethical judgments that would be necessary and sufficient to assert such an identity.

Among the positive or technical studies of income distribution, it is difficult to find many that begin with a consistent set of assumptions about individuals' objective functions, initial endowments, and the relative prices confronting them, which then deduce choices and how these will interact to produce market outcomes, especially in the form of income distributions. The prime candidate appears to be recent work extending the human capital model to explain the distribution of labor incomes, especially by Mincer (1970, 1974), Chiswick (1974), and Tinbergen (1975).

Other technical work is predominantly statistical in that it searches for functional forms that best fit income data, or it examines the properties of various summary statistics describing dispersion, or it defines and produces the underlying data. Examples of function fitting would be the Aitchison and Brown (1957) use of the size distribution as an example of a log-normal distribution; more recent work by Metcalf (1974) is another instance. The large number of models that make use of chance variation and ability distributions as the basic mechanism behind income distributions may be assigned to this category; examples include Gibrat (1931), Champernowne (1953), Rutherford (1955), Mandelbrot (1962), and Pryor (1973).

Closely related is the search for summary statistics that best capture the distributions, including Champernowne (1974), Atkinson (1970), Elteto and Frigyes (1968), and Kondor (1971). Also related are recent applications of the regression model to the Gini coefficient by Kakwani and Podder (1973), and the evaluation of alternative procedures to calculate the Gini coefficient by Gastwirth (1972).

Perhaps the most important technical concern of all involves the data base, since the observed "facts" are recorded via particular measurement procedures (Morgenstern 1963). These procedures are described in the main sources of income data—the 1940, 1950, 1960, and 1970 Population Censuses, BLS Surveys of Consumer Expenditures, Annual Current Population Surveys of the Census Bureau, and the Michigan Surveys of Consumer Finances. Other examples in this area would be Kravis (1962); Budd, Radner, and Hinrichs (1973); Brady (1951); Projector and Bretz (1972); Goldsmith et al. (1954); and Henle (1972). Studies that have examined the sensitivity of distributions to alternative conventions, such as whether to include capital gains, impute a flow of income to consumer durables, or measure on an annual basis or a longer period, include certain volumes of the National Bureau's Conference on Research in Income and Wealth (National Bureau of Economic Research 1951; Soltow 1969; Smith 1975), as well as Brady (1965), Schultz (1972), and Paglin (1975). Some studies have used the distribution of income as an independent variable to explain consumption expenditures (Blinder 1975). Others have made it the dependent variable and have explained the distribution of income on the basis of income levels (Kuznets 1955; Adelman and Morris 1973; Paukert 1973; Fishlow 1972); as well as other variables (Lydall 1968; Schultz 1969; Mincer and Chiswick 1972; Metcalf 1972).

Administrative efforts to define and measure poverty, from the English poor laws through the city worker budget to the War on Poverty, are examples of the predominantly normative literature. In this area, the Institute for Survey Research at the University of Michigan has been important (Morgan et al. 1962), and recently studies relating income to "need" have emanated from the Institute for Research on Poverty at the University of Wisconsin (Watts 1967). Wiles (1974) apparently would also prefer to place his work in this category, as would Meade (1964).

Almost no empirical work has been explicitly egalitarian in recent times, but this has not been true of theoretical work. The dominance of egalitarianism can be traced to Jeremy Bentham some two centuries ago, who specified that the appropriate goal of a society is to maximize the satisfactions of its citizens, and that a given total income yields the greatest aggregate satisfaction when it is equally divided. The implication of equal division rested upon assumptions that were assaulted by the new welfare economics, primarily that numerical utilities could be assigned to the satisfactions enjoyed by individuals (cardinal utility functions), that the value assigned to different individuals could be appropriately added (interpersonal comparisons), and that all utility functions were identical and had the property of diminishing marginal utility of income. Lerner (1944) attempted to preserve the Benthamite result of equal income but to weaken an assumption by invoking the principle of "equal ignorance" about the efficiency of different individuals as pleasure machines. This was criticized by Friedman (1953b, pp. 310–11), who pointed out that if we discovered that a hundred persons are enormously more efficient pleasure machines than any others, then to maximize aggregate utility, each of those with a huge thirst for market goods would have to be given incomes ten thousand times larger than the incomes of the next most efficient pleasure machines.

More recently, the literature on decision making under uncertainty has been transferred to the normative literature on income distribution. Risk aversion is a commonly accepted property of individual preferences in portfolio selection, occupational choice, etc. If this property is also assumed of a class of social welfare functions and, further, if social choices are over a set of income distributions, ceteris paribus, the results of risk analysis can be transferred in toto. The egalitarian nature of this spate of literature is obvious since income dispersion is identical to risk for individuals, that is to say, income dispersion is a "bad." Examples are Sen (1973), Mirlees (1971), and Sheshinski (1972). Rawls's work (1971) might be summarized as advocating the most extreme type of risk aversion, minimax, which implies the choice of that distribution with the highest expected value for the low income, ignoring all other characteristics of the distributions.

Related work includes simulations seeking a revealed social welfare function in government behavior (Fair 1971; Cooter and Helpman 1974). In the same spirit have been benefit–cost analyses that specifically introduce distributive weights into program evaluations (Haveman 1965; Mera 1969; and Weisbrod 1968).

Plan of the Book

This book falls among the technical studies. It explores the response of measured income inequality to a more comprehensive definition of household income, in particular, one that includes the benefits and burdens of government at all levels. In this analysis, we follow the practice, more or less, of a line of studies by Musgrave et al. (1951), Adler (1951), Conrad (1954), Musgrave, Case, and Leonard (1974), Reynolds and Smolensky (1974), and Pechman and Okner (1974) in the United States; and studies of other countries by Clark (1937), Barna (1945), Brown (1973), Schnitzer (1974), and Dodge (1975). We do not, however, intend to address the same questions.

The empirical exercises undertaken in this literature are usually intended to answer the question: What impact does the fisc have in redistributing income? In chapter 2, we explore what must be known to answer that question, by setting down alternative definitions of redistribution. Chapter 2 is by no means a complete discussion of the difficulties, but it is sufficient to establish that the question probably cannot be satisfactorily answered. We then turn to a different, answerable question in chapter 3. There we ask: What happened to the size distribution of income in the United States between 1950 and 1970, when household income is defined so as to include the benefits and burdens of all levels of government? Chapters 4 and 5 present extensive comparisons of final income distributions under alternative assumptions about the incidence of taxes and expenditures. Chapter 6 discusses some experimental results involving artificial government budgets. Chapter 7 summarizes the major findings. The data that permit others to reconsider the issues are contained in the Appendixes.

One question remains: Why have we invested our time in studying post-fisc distributions of income? This book compares size distributions of income in 1950, 1961, and 1970 after allocating all government taxes and expenditures across households (final income). The motivation is to detect changes in final income distributions over two decades by constructing a systematic, intertemporal comparison. But is this any more important to know than it would have been 100 years ago? We believe the answer is yes. Interest in economic inequality has traditionally been directed at the distribution of money income, with related distributions like that for non-human wealth or consumption expenditures relegated to a secondary role. However, even these distributions comprise only a subset of the dimensions of economic welfare, not to mention a more broadly conceived distribution of welfare. For example, we might define economic welfare for an individual to include his present value endowment of "nonmarket" goods, like government services, unpaid services performed in the home, leisure, natural environment, and work satisfaction. Scitovsky (1973) speculates that these goods are more equally distributed than money income, except for work satisfaction, which he feels is positively correlated with money income, thus adding to inequality.

Inclusion of the public sector in income distribution is a step in the direction of a more comprehensive measure of economic inequality. It is obviously still a partial measure but even a partial answer is not without interest. It seems especially important to account for the distribution of public services over a period when the ratio of government expenditures to Net National Product (NNP) has grown from 20 percent in 1950 to 35 percent in 1970. Put in less familiar terms, the private sector has decreased from 80 to 65 percent of NNP in the last two decades. Finally, we believe that measuring the change between years makes fewer demands upon the conventional techniques of aggregate fiscal incidence studies; but let us defer this discussion until later chapters.

Postscript

It goes without saying, except in an occasional aside, that the driving force behind much of the work on the size distribution, no matter how technical, is ideological. It is difficult to explain the great quantity of recent work on any other grounds.

Most empirical work is associated with some construct central to an important aspect of economic theory. The consumption function, the demand for money equation, the term structure of interest rates, the concavity of lifetime earnings profiles, or floating exchange rates are examples. The size distribution of income, however, is distantly related to the human capital model, and to a conjecture by Kuznets (1955), and that is about all. Since the moments of the size distribution are neither dependent nor independent variables in any significant analytical model, it seems reasonable to look elsewhere for the motivating energy.

Our experience in presenting these results to small informal groups suggests that the interest aroused relates to what may be called "academic gossip," although the most accurate word we know to describe it is the Yiddish "tsitser." A tsitser is a kibitzer, a habitual sympathizer and bystander who does not participate but "who is always going 'Ts! Ts!' or 'Tsk! Tsk!' or even 'Tchk! Tchk!'" (Rosten 1968, p. 411).

The tsitser is common enough around economics, but he is drawn most naturally to the size distribution where, after all, we have known since Pareto that, despite a quibble here and there, the more things change, the more they remain the same. Modern liberals would like the data to show declining income inequality, except in their masochistic bouts. Radicals apparently would like the data to show increasing income inequality but would presumably be satisfied to find that government, despite its rhetoric, leaves inequality unaltered. Conservatives are gleeful over the failures of the social engineers, but they would still like to be able to confidently assert that growth in income and more equality of income are positively correlated. Perhaps our findings will nourish the tsitsers for some time to come.

2
Alternative Definitions of Income Redistribution

When no tactful answer seems to suffice and the . . . probing goes on, the only solution is to be quite frank. Say, without getting angry, . . . I don't feel willing to answer. If he then takes offense, he deserves to. [Amy Vanderbilt 1963, p. 216]

In recent years, much has been written about the technical difficulties inherent in measuring the effects of all levels of government upon the size distribution of income. How income redistribution ought to be defined—the most basic of all the technical difficulties—has not received much detailed consideration, however, perhaps because the theoretical literature offers little direct guidance. This chapter is, thus, devoted to a discussion of four conceptually distinct ways in which redistribution can be defined.[1] It shows that none of them has much operational value. It argues further that the general equilibrium problem involved in giving empirical meaning to any of the definitions may well be intractable, and that we probably cannot either measure what slice of income can be ascribed to government redistribution, or isolate how government has changed the economic position of the different income classes.

Any measure of *re*distribution involves comparing a distribution of money income "before" certain taxes, transfers, and other government expenditures with a distribution "after." This implies breaking into the general interdependence of public and private decisions with some counterfactual to measure the "before" distribution.[2] The question becomes: Which is the appropriate counterfactual? This is the dimension on which our four alternative general equilibrium definitions of redistribution differ. We

---

[1] This chapter is based upon Behrens and Smolensky (1973).

[2] Perhaps it should be noted that the preponderance of "redistributive" studies are of a particular program or program change. These studies generally take as their counterfactual the status quo ante. For examples, see Boulding and Pfaff (1972).

examine the implications of these different definitions of redistribution so as to make the nature of the normative choice among alternative definitions more explicit.

The first section of the chapter indicates the nature of the problems involved in defining redistribution. Then the four different definitions we have chosen to discuss are compared and evaluated, and the conceptual and empirical roadblocks in the way of efforts to operationalize them are discussed. An algebraic comparison is in Appendix A.

The Concept of Redistribution

In our efforts to clarify the concept of redistribution by government, let us first discuss what the appropriate unit of analysis is. The basic unit in economics is the individual rather than a class of individuals, whether the classes are defined by income, benefits received, taxes paid, or in some other way. Individuals generally live in groups and pool their incomes, however, so economists also often find it convenient to examine families, households, or spending units. Little is known about the factors that determine whether and how individuals form multiperson units,[3] but for our purposes this problem can be ignored, because we can treat the decision unit which is an individual and the decision unit which is a multiperson household as synonymous. To posit the existence of a consistent preference structure for a kinship group requires a bold aggregation procedure, but we shall do it here because it is not central to our present argument.[4] When we use "individual," therefore, we mean to include any income-earning and income-spending unit.

The second clarification we want to make concerns what shall be included in government—more specifically, the question of which government activities affecting the income distribution shall be said to redistribute income. Buchanan (1970) has been willing to conceive of a pure market economy. Under this conception, all influences of government upon individual incomes might be taken to be redistributive. It is more usual, however, to argue that some government activity is necessary for the efficient functioning of a market economy, if only to define and enforce private property rights.[5] This immediately leads to a complication. Securing one set

---

[3] Becker (1973, 1974) has made a beginning on the issue.

[4] Individuals are often grouped by primary income for empirical work, and redistribution defined as a vector of average effects by income class. However, since average results can always be derived from individual results, we only consider individual effects in this chapter.

[5] As Adam Smith (1950, p. 203) wrote, "The acquisition of valuable and extensive property, therefore, necessarily requires the establishment of civil government. Where there is no property, or at least none that exceeds the value of two or three days labour, civil government is not so necessary."

of ownership rights rather than another can obviously affect the distribution of income and wealth. For example, consider the generation of factor income which is superficially independent of government. The distribution of factor income can be decomposed into three elements: (1) the distribution of resource ownership per period, (2) the prices received per unit of factor input, and (3) the rate of usage per period, or the amounts rented.

Expansion or attenuation of property rights, which depend critically upon government behavior, are quickly reflected in prices and quantities in factor markets, at least if markets function well. We shall abstract from this complication by assuming that government exists and operates on a scale sufficient to secure some initial configuration of ownership rights that remains unchanged throughout the analysis. Under this simplifying assumption, then, government action can create individual gains and losses in two general ways: (*a*) price and quantity effects in factor markets; and (*b*) price and quantity effects in product markets. With respect to factor markets, government action can change the net receipt stream, or market value, of factor services owned by an individual. Levying or increasing a tax on labor earnings lowers net receipts to owners of labor services, at least initially, and a tax levied (removed) on housing lowers (raises) asset values to home owners. Individuals who own none of the assets in question realize no immediate effects unless the government has engaged in frequent, unpredictable changes in the rules of the game, which would tend to lower all asset values. All government effects on factor markets, whether intended or not, whether due to demand or supply behavior, can be considered within this general framework.

In product markets, government can change the attainable consumption set facing different individuals. Government action can directly transfer income among individuals, change the relative prices of existing goods (directly or indirectly), introduce a good not previously available, or eliminate a good previously available. Examples of the effects of government on relative prices are below-cost pricing in higher education, passenger trains, and irrigation water; or the higher prices due to the behavior of regulatory agencies like the ICC, FTC, and CAB.

Introduction of new goods occurs in cases where private markets would never produce a perfect substitute. An example might be primary education, where it is sometimes argued that private schools would never produce the core of common values conveyed by more homogeneous public school systems. Perhaps more persuasive examples are national defense or the court systems. Government can also prohibit or eliminate goods that the private market would otherwise provide—for example, marijuana, pornography, margarine, and firecrackers—at various times and in various places. None of the effects on individual consumption sets have to be symmetric across all individuals. For example, prices for public medical care can be reduced only for the "poor," or cigarette sales prohibited only to those under age 16.

All such factor and product market changes brought about by government jointly determine a new consumption set attainable by each individual. This is what we mean by the net distributive effect of a government program. In principle, we could even determine the individual welfare result of all proposed changes in the parameters describing government behavior. Each individual could be offered a choice between government actions A and B. Both options would be considered in terms of present value differences between attainable bundles in a world of complete information and complete markets. Revealed choices by each individual would allow us to describe which individuals would be worse off or better off if either A or B were adopted. Policy options could be extended indefinitely, and each individual could rank them ordinally, in the same fashion that individuals are assumed to be able to completely order private goods.

We have no obvious way of aggregating across individuals to arrive at a collective ranking of government policies, however, as Arrow (1951) has demonstrated so famously. Among the many aggregation procedures that might be used to achieve collective rankings, market exchange is a particularly interesting device because it permits cardinal, interpersonal comparisons and leads to a natural definition of an efficient government action. Consider again the comparison of two government actions, A and B. We could ask all individuals: How much are you willing to pay to avoid B? Some would be willing to pay large amounts, some would be indifferent to A and B, and some, who prefer B, would be willing to pay negative amounts. Alternatively we could ask: How much would you be willing to accept in compensation for the adoption of program B and remain at least as well off as you are now? Unless income effects were large, these two answers would be about the same for all individuals and they would be the same in the aggregate. The action receiving the highest net value would be adopted by an efficient government. If compensation were actually paid, it would also represent Pareto improvement, because at least one person would be better off and no one worse off. This is the unanimity principle of Wicksell (1958) in another guise.

Income redistribution due to government can thus be defined as the change in the real income of individuals when the parameters that describe government are changed. (This definition does not confine the redistributive effects of government to a zero sum game or "purely redistributive" policies, because aggregate income and mean income can also change.) We can now narrow our inquiry somewhat from the abstract and very general discussion so far, by focusing on the objectives of studies of government benefits and burdens.

Studies of budget incidence traditionally are interested in vertical equity, which ambiguously states that unequals should be treated unequally. In practice, this means grouping individuals into annual income classes and asking whether taxes and expenditures are proportional, regressive, or progressive with respect to current income. Given this interest in vertical equity, the primary income distribution, which means the vector of individual incomes arising from the assumed ("before" government) counterfactual, must be an appropriate index for ranking individuals in terms of who are equals and who are unequals. Once the primary distribution is determined, the redistributive effect of government on each individual is the difference between his primary income and his final income, which is the income he receives under existing governmental parameters. Redistribution can then be defined as a vector which shows the difference between primary and final income for each individual and can be evaluated on criteria of both vertical and horizontal equity.[6] In other words, the problem is choosing an origin, or proper set of counterfactual parameters. This is an issue, as we pointed out above, that has so far been neglected.

Alternative Definitions

To simplify the discussion, the term "government" will refer throughout to all levels of government combined, on the assumption that vertical and horizontal equity are objectives of the national government. If local governments pursue their own redistributive objectives, then new issues are introduced. Eapen (1966), who advocates allowing state governments to make equity decisions, has suggested that the federal government rank

---

[6] The theoretical literature in public finance has often been vague on this point. For example, horizontal and vertical equity are usually discussed as though only a proper definition of income is necessary to define equals and unequals, given the unit of analysis. The comparative-static dimension of the problem, i.e., the necessity of choosing a counterfactual, is generally left in the background. For example, see Richard A. Musgrave (1959, chap. 8). A. C. Pigou (1928, p. 58) explicitly adopts the zero government counterfactual but he offers no justification for this choice.

The definition of redistribution need not be confined to changes in government parameters when the objective is to measure vertical equity. For example, one assumption governing the counterfactual could be that there are no private transfers. However, it may still be said that the resulting definition of redistribution is redistribution *by government*. If the counterfactual defines equals and unequals, and government is charged with the responsibility of achieving vertical and horizontal equality, then the effects of private transfers can be attributed to government on the grounds that it can take into account the predicted level of private transfers in designing redistributive policies. Only changes in government parameters are involved in the definitions of redistribution discussed here.

persons by their income *net* of the effects (burdens and benefits) of state governments. However, subnational political jurisdictions may have no effective redistributive power because migration is low cost, in which case only the national government can be said to be effective.

As a further simplification, the difficult problem of defining the nonfiscal policies appropriate to a primary "before" distribution will be handled by assuming in all cases (1) that all private markets are perfectly competitive, (2) that the nonfiscal policies prevailing in the counterfactual are those appropriate for defining equals and unequals, and (3) that the same nonfiscal policies govern the final distribution. Nonfiscal policies can, therefore, be ignored. Similarly, we eliminate consideration of the redistributive effects of stabilization policy by assuming a neoclassical system of balanced budgets, full employment output, and stable price level.

The same definition of the final distribution of income is assumed in all cases. It is the distribution of after-tax factor income plus transfers and benefits of all final government services. The benefits of general government services (which include any taxpayer benefits accruing from transfer programs) and recipient benefits of in-kind transfers are all valued at their marginal valuation to each individual as given by his demand curve for each service. This treatment of government benefits is consistent with the valuation of private goods. The final distribution is that existing under actual government parameters, that is, parameters prevailing in the time period for which redistribution is measured.

The definitions of redistribution that follow result from alternative a priori views of the appropriate definition of the *primary* distribution.[7]

Case I

The most commonly assumed counterfactual in the literature is an economy in which there is neither government expenditures nor taxes. This zero government case, a much criticized counterfactual, includes all effects of government fiscal activities in redistribution (Prest 1955). The zero government counterfactual (which hereafter refers to a zero budget since nonfiscal policies are ignored) constitutes our case I. In this case, the private-sector distribution of factor incomes is taken to satisfactorily define equals and unequals. Any and all changes in this private-sector distribution resulting from any and all taxes and expenditures of government is then viewed as its income redistribution consequences. This is consistent with the Gillespie (1965) approach.

[7] A more formal algebraic statement is in Appendix A.

Case II

Our second case defines the primary distribution of income (the distribution that defines equals and unequals) as that arising from the private sector *plus* the allocative activities of the public sector (including recipient benefits from efficient transfers). Allocative activities of government are defined as all those activities which increase the efficient use of resources.

One such distribution is that which would obtain if the government used only marginal benefit taxation. This is the primary distribution we shall use to illustrate case II because it has the simplifying property of arising from a Lindahl equilibrium. A Lindahl equilibrium combines the provision of private goods through the perfectly competitive private markets with the provision of collective goods according to a Lindahl solution, given a distribution of initial endowments (Foley 1970).[8]

This primary distribution differs from that which would prevail in case I because, although benefits received by each individual are balanced by taxes paid in Lindahl equilibrium, factor incomes may have also been altered in going from zero government to the Lindahl equilibrium. This change in factor income is often ignored, incorrectly implying that the provision of public goods by a Lindahl solution involves no alteration in individual incomes (Aaron and McGuire 1970).

Case II redistribution, therefore, excludes the effects on factor income which arise from the allocative activities of government. Any redistribution that does take place in case II comes about primarily in three ways.[9] First, the taxes actually levied to finance the purely allocative expenditures of government may deviate from marginal benefit taxation. Second, government may undertake exhaustive expenditures not justified on efficiency grounds to provide factor income to certain subgroups of the population. Third, the government may make transfers, either in cash or in kind, to certain groups in the population at the expense of other groups. We shall refer to these three methods of redistributing income as the "redistributive policies" of government.

In defining case II redistribution, as we have seen, a distinction must be made between the allocative and the redistributive policies of government—a distinction which is eliminated in the Pareto-optimal redistribution litera-

[8] Lindahl himself would probably not define this as the primary distinction. He would probably define redistribution as the alteration in initial endowments *before* the allocation of resources to the public sector, when the latter are provided according to a Lindahl solution (Lindahl 1958).

[9] A fourth source of redistribution is unintended inefficiencies in the provision of government services. These are not formally different, however, from inefficiencies which are deliberately created to redistribute factor income and are not considered separately in our analysis.

ture. To the extent that individual taxpayers benefit from redistributive policies, the provision of these programs may be viewed as collective consumption on the part of these taxpayers. Redistribution can produce a Pareto improvement if the utility of certain individuals, or their consumption of specific commodities, enters the utility functions of other individuals or if the income distribution itself enters individual utility functions (Hochman and Rodgers 1969; Thurow 1971).[10]

But an element of Pareto-optimal redistribution exits whenever a redistributive action by government generates nonrecipient benefits. Under the assumption that (1) nonrecipient beneficiaries are taxed according to the marginal benefits they receive from the government actions, and (2) benefits to recipients are not taxed, efficient transfers are more appropriately defined as an allocative activity of government. Under case II, therefore, efficient transfers will be included in the primary distribution. Note that this procedure excludes both efficient recipient benefits and nonrecipient benefits from the definition of redistribution.

It is conceivable that all government transfers are efficient in this sense— that the portion of exhaustive expenditures not justified on other allocative grounds constitutes efficient redistribution, and that individual taxes collected for these transfers and other expenditures are, in fact, equal to what would be assessed in a regime of marginal benefit taxation. If these conditions held simultaneously, the primary distribution would be identical with the final distribution; and, by definition, government would not be redistributing.

Case III

The fundamental definition for case III is the same as case II—that is, the primary distribution of income is defined as arising from the private sector plus the allocative activities of the public sector. The difference between cases II and III lies in the treatment of recipient benefits, which in case III are all excluded from the primary distributions.

In our case II discussion, the primary distribution was described as that which would prevail if only benefit taxation were used. The provision of efficient transfers, however, may be said to violate this principle of taxation. Although the nonrecipient beneficiaries are taxed according to their marginal benefits, transfer recipients receive benefits which are not taxed. This consideration suggests removing the recipient benefits from the

---

[10] The scope for government to discover and administer a potentially beneficial reallocation is more probable under conditions of poorly defined and enforced private property rights and/ or high contracting costs for voluntary agreements, because the gains from efficient transfers would otherwise be exploited privately.

primary distribution and including them in the redistributive effects of government.

Case III is consistent with Lampman's view that redistribution is the receipt of "consumer-power income" by individuals that does not correspond to their "producer-contribution" (Lampman 1969). Case III differs from case I (zero government counterfactual), therefore, only in that it excludes the effect of government allocative activities on factor incomes from the definition of redistribution, including it in the primary distribution defining equals and unequals.

Case IV

A fourth definition of redistribution (Behrens and Smolensky 1973) specifies that the primary distribution be an optimal one in terms of some social welfare function. In the counterfactual which defines the primary distribution, the government engages in allocative activities and carries out redistributive policies on the basis of some explicit ability-to-pay criterion, thereby achieving an intended optimum. The case IV definition requires that the primary distribution identify equals and unequals, and in this it does not differ from the other three cases. In addition, however, it necessitates making an explicit judgment about vertical equity by requiring the choice of a specific ability-to-pay criterion. The definition of equals and unequals may be based on the case I, case II, and case III, or any other counterfactual. This is then altered on the basis of the ability-to-pay criterion to produce the case IV counterfactual.

As in the other cases, redistribution in case IV is simply the difference between the final and primary distributions. Given a definition of equals and unequals, case IV redistribution is the difference between the actual fiscal treatment individuals receive and the way they would be treated if the specified optimum distribution were achieved.

Evaluation of the Definitions

Differences among these concepts of redistribution lie along two dimensions. What distinguishes case I from both case II and case III is the conception of allocative activities of government. The other major difference, which differentiates case IV from both cases II and III, and from case I, is the tax principle invoked to define the primary distribution.

The common acceptance of the distribution of private incomes for defining equals and unequals, as in case I (the zero government counterfactual), appears to rest upon two principal rationales, both of which ignore the components of government activity that constitute production of efficient amounts of collective goods. The first rationale is a normative judgment that individuals *should* be ranked by their factor incomes because it is the appropriate index of equality in applying the principle of horizontal equity. The second is a taxonomic view that all effects of government activity *should* be included in any overall measure of redistribution.

Even if factor income is chosen as an explicit index for defining equals and unequals, numerous practical difficulties ensue in any attempt to measure it, such as the definition of the income unit, nonmonetary income, and so on. There is also, however, a serious conceptual objection to using individual factor income in the world of zero government as the primary distribution against which to measure government redistribution efforts. The allocative activities of an efficient government will, in general, change the rank order of the "equals" and "unequals" established in the case of zero government, because individual factor incomes will be changed by those activities. Another way of stating this is that factor owners are not receiving their social marginal products under zero government. Thus, if the normative objective is to rank people by the value of the social marginal products of the factors they own, then the counterfactual must include the allocative activities of both the private and public sectors.

The second rationale—that all effects of government should be included in the definition of redistribution—may have intuitive appeal at first. It becomes less attractive when it is shown to imply an asymmetric treatment of the allocative activities of the private and public sectors. For example, if the steel industry were to disappear, the incomes of some factor owners would be lowered and those of others would rise. The consequences of steel production for the distribution of income, however, are not included in the case I definition of redistribution since they simply contribute to the formation of the private distribution (assuming, for the sake of argument, that all derived demands for steel are private). Case I redistribution does, in contrast, include the redistributive consequences of the production of nuclear submarines, simply because the demand for this commodity emanates from the public rather than the private sector.

This asymmetry in treatment of the public and private sectors does not arise in cases II and III, because all consequences of the pursuit of allocative efficiency are excluded, by definition, from redistribution. This seems reasonable. If the allocative function of government is viewed only as a use of income by individuals to buy collectively consumed goods and services, which are paid for at "market" prices, there seems to be no compelling reason to include the distributional effects of merely allocating resources to the public sector, but to exclude the effects of allocating resources to particular uses in the private sector. This argument suggests that case II and case III definitions of redistribution are preferable to the case I concept if individuals are to be ranked by their market incomes.[11]

Most theoretical and empirical studies of redistribution do not give an explicit reason for using the zero government (case I) counterfactual. To the two rationales already mentioned, there should be added a third possible rationale for its use. This is the value judgment that persons should be ranked by their private market incomes, whether or not these are equal to marginal social products.[12] This type of specific value judgment, of course, cannot be rejected on logical or empirical grounds. The asymmetric treatment of the allocative activities of the private and public sectors, however, still would seem to reduce its appeal as a counterfactual.

The case II and case III definitions of redistribution have more theoretical appeal than a counterfactual of zero government, because they do not count the allocative effects of efficient government as redistributive. The interesting distinction between them depends on whether acceptance of transfers is assumed to be part of the recipient's marginal product. If this interpretation is accepted, case II is consistent with a strict ranking of owners by the marginal products of the factors owned. Pareto-optimal transfers yield benefits to some taxpayers, and the fact that the recipients are not taxed for the benefits is then irrelevant because they are engaging in a "productive activity" rather than receiving untaxed benefits from govern-

---

[11] That there are at least two definitions of redistribution (case I and case II) based on market counterfactuals which exclude the effects of governmental allocative activities may also resolve an issue that has arisen in the incidence literature.

Musgrave (1959, pp. 213–15) has argued that it is not very meaningful to measure the distributional consequences of the budget. Such a measure includes the effects of expenditures which he asserts are largely unintended. Musgrave would like to remove these effects, but doing so and measuring only the effects of taxes would force the analysis to examine an unbalanced budget change. We have shown, however, that the redistributive effects of allocative expenditures can be conceptually removed from the measure of redistribution in a balanced-budget way, by assigning these expenditures to the counterfactual on the assumption that they are financed by marginal benefit taxes of the same amount.

[12] At least one study of redistribution seems to be based on the idea that persons should be ranked by their private incomes, per se. Tibor Barna defines redistribution as a deviation from a system of "neutral finance," i.e., "from a state in which the distribution of incomes is left unaltered by government" (1945, p. 11). His definition derives from an earlier discussion by F. C. Benham (1934), who apparently saw neutral finance as a means of fulfilling the social compact. Benham's definition of neutral finance was that system which individuals would voluntarily choose (not necessarily equivalent to Barna's definition), and he viewed all deviations from that system as inequitable. Once it is admitted, however, that deviations from "neutral finance" may be desirable, and Barna clearly thinks they are, the philosophy of government as a social compact has been rejected. There appears to be no reason why government should, on the basis of this philosophy, rank individuals by their private-market incomes, if it may violate the social compact in achieving equity. The significance of the social contract has recently been revived by John Rawls (1971).

ment. In other words, if transfer recipients are analogous to children and pets in that their services as dependents are demanded by other individuals, case II is consistent with marginal benefit taxation in every dimension. Whether this kind of phenomenon is empirically relevant is unknown but it does serve to emphasize the distinction between case II and case III.

Case III involves an asymmetric treatment of the public and private sectors in one respect. When Pareto-optimal redistribution is carried out in the public sector, the benefits to recipients are considered part of redistribution. When the private sector provides such redistribution, however, recipient benefits are excluded. Lampman (1969) has implied that the concept of redistribution should be extended to private-sector transactions, including transactions in the insurance sector. If the case III definition is used it might be preferable to modify it by including recipient benefits of private transfers and thus use a more "global" definition of redistribution.

The differences among the case I counterfactual and cases II and III turn on alternative views of the appropriate ranking of individuals. By contrast, the case IV counterfactual takes the definition of equals and unequals as given and asks what concept of redistribution best characterizes the degree to which vertical equity is achieved. A measure of redistribution based on any of the case I, II, or III counterfactuals (or others) will show whether the differences between unequals have narrowed, widened, or remained unchanged. An all-too-common interpretation of such results is that progressivity must represent movement toward an optimum. Perfect equality of incomes is thus used as an implicit standard, even while it is explicitly rejected as the ultimate equity objective.

The case IV counterfactual has the virtue of being very explicit about its normative character, as well as being readily interpretable. Any redistribution by government (other than what is specified in the social welfare function and therefore already included in the primary distribution) represents deviations from a specified optimum and is therefore "harmful." This can, of course, produce some semantic confusion. In most studies of budget incidence, progressivity in the fiscal system commonly has the connotation of taking from the rich and giving to the poor. Suppose we accept the usual "Robin Hood" view that redistribution from the rich to the poor is "good." On this view, the case IV definition labels a failure by government to redistribute income among rich and poor until all incomes are exactly equal as a redistribution of income from the poor to the rich. This may reveal the threadbare nature of the case IV counterfactual,[13] but it does emphasize the kinds of normative judgments that become involved in what is conceptually labeled redistribution.

---

[13] As Voltaire wrote, "The best is the enemy of the good."

Conclusion

We have considered four alternative definitions of income redistribution that might be used in empirical studies designed to show the extent to which vertical equity is achieved through government. All definitions are in terms of comparisons of long-run equilibria arising from actual government policies and some specific counterfactual. If analysis of vertical equity is the objective, the distribution of income arising from the before-redistribution counterfactual must appropriately rank individuals as equals or unequals. The zero government counterfactual (case I) ignores the role of government in achieving allocative efficiency and, therefore, does not rank individuals by social marginal products. Cases II and III include the allocative activities of government in the counterfactual, although they differ in their treatment of Pareto-optimal redistribution. Finally, the case IV concept defines redistribution as deviations of the actual distribution from a specified optimum.

These definitions by no means exhaust the theoretical possibilities. Indeed, they illustrate the wide range of interpretations which might be given to the notion of redistribution. From an empirical point of view, none of the definitions has much operational value.

Long-run incomes in a world of zero government are unknown and perhaps unknowable in modern economies so far removed from zero governments. A zero government budget is an extreme, theoretically inappropriate, conceptual experiment, particularly because the pre-fisc distribution already reflects a host of market adjustments to government behavior. This led Cannan (Prest 1955, p. 244) justifiably to comment in 1927 that such a statistical "inquiry is a will-o-the-wisp" and "absolutely useless." In practice, analysts assume that the distribution of "pretax" market incomes would be no different if government were zero. The weakness of this interpretation hardly needs pointing out.

The conceptual bases of the three other alternatives we have discussed are stronger. Their empirical content, however, is no greater. Cases II and III depend critically upon knowing the pattern of benevolence in an economy of millions of individuals. Presumably, government ignores malevolent feelings of its citizen consumers, and only taxes and transfers in response to charitable demands. Even so, knowledge of the size and pattern of an efficient government tax and expenditure scheme is unattainable. The case IV definition fares as poorly. What constitutes an optimum distribution or the "best" initial distribution is, of course, conceptually unknown and certainly cannot then have an empirical representation. If this problem had been resolved by now, welfare economics would no longer have a question to investigate.

The burden of this chapter has been to show that it is not sensible to try to discover the aggregate redistributive impact of government in a given year by assigning burdens and benefits to income classes in the conventional way. Subsequent chapters, therefore, will trace changes in the size distribution of income over time, when income is defined to include the benefits and burdens of government at all levels. To pursue this objective we estimate the distribution of final output using comparable incidence assumptions for each year but with the new amounts of income, taxes, and expenditures for each year.

The basic criticism of numerical studies of this kind carries less force against our objective because only the change (if any) in a more comprehensive measure of the size distribution of income is at issue. Our calculations need not be formally correct in all dimensions but must only yield an unbiased approximation of the changes in final distributions over time. Measuring changes between years makes fewer demands upon the conventional technique than trying to measure the size and nature of redistribution in a single year for three reasons.

First, it obviates the need for a hypothetical counterfactual. Conceptually, the final distribution of income is viewed as the simultaneous outcome of both public and private activity even though the calculations are performed in a stepwise sequence which suggests independence.

The two remaining reasons for being somewhat more comfortable with the technique concern biases in the data. It is likely that (1) any biases are in the same direction in both years, and (2) the biases are likely to be of similar magnitude within the range of distributive change in the U.S. during relatively short time intervals. If these two conditions hold, they are sufficient to ensure that any measured, sizable distributive change by income class will be of the appropriate direction and magnitude. That these two conditions hold in this instance cannot be demonstrated with certainty, but the example of Social Security suggests that the intertemporal comparison may be unbiased even though the bias is large in each year.

The Social Security system provides an excellent illustration of the bias resulting from using an accounting period of one year (Browning 1973; Feldstein 1974). A single-year accounting period exaggerates the size of government redistribution by almost any definition of redistribution. The costs and benefits of many (perhaps all) public activities vary with a household's stage in the life cycle. They also vary with current income and other variables, but the life cycle is especially visible in the Social Security case.[14]

---

[14] Of course there are other distributive issues associated with the Social Security system, such as any effect on the rate of aggregate income growth, private savings, interest rates, and so on.

The exaggerated effect that the age distribution produces in the conventional measure of redistribution by Social Security emerges in the following way: In each year, as measured, cash payments are highly concentrated at the low end of the income distribution. Payroll taxes are roughly proportional over the middle portion of the income distribution and smaller at both tails. Obviously, this allocation is very different from what would be observed in a wealth or permanent income framework. The present value of lifetime benefits would be distributed somewhat like the present value of payments, and only the smaller amount of redistribution inherent in the loose connection between taxes and benefits would enter the redistributive measure. Taking year-to-year differences, however, cancels out much of this bias because the redistributive effects of the system are approximately equally exaggerated in each year.

Measuring distributions only on a flow basis probably exaggerates the redistribution of much government activity (e.g., education, debt finance, unemployment compensation) relative to some appropriate, lifetime cohort analysis—although this assertion cannot be stated confidently, since the cohort approach has never been implemented.

The argument that an intertemporal comparison of final distributions compromises with economic theory less severely than do comparisons within a given year is, it must be admitted, somewhat ingenuous, since we shall, despite our reservations on theoretical grounds, speak of the redistribution of income by expenditure and tax categories within a year. In a strictly arithmetic sense, differences between initial and final income inequality in a single year are attributable to certain taxes or expenditures, and we shall make such attributions. It is true that this kind of disaggregation ignores all indirect behavioral effects due to a program—effects that might present an entirely different impression if they were known—but it nonetheless makes for useful speculations so long as the limitations of the comparisons are borne in mind. Our intent, however, remains to concentrate attention on the changing distribution of final income.

3

Empirical Procedures

Whether inequality is actually increasing or diminishing in a particular community during a particular period of time is, of course, a statistical question, which may be answered independently of general argument regarding economic cause and effect, provided, first, that the relevant income statistics are known, and second, that a measure of inequality is agreed upon and applied to these statistics. But, in fact, the relevant statistics are in most cases very imperfectly known, and the difficulty of agreeing upon a measure of inequality is much greater than is commonly realized.
[Hugh Dalton; Brady 1951, pp. 351–52]

The General Procedure

Generating a post-fisc distribution in any year involves three major steps:

(1) Constructing an income base or pre-fisc distribution,
(2) adding government expenditures by income class to the pre-fisc distribution, and
(3) subtracting taxes by income class from the pre-fisc distribution.

The procedure can be compactly stated in matrix form as

$$\mathbf{c} = \mathbf{m} + \mathbf{gB} - \mathbf{xT} \qquad (3\text{-}1)$$

In expanded form:

$$[c_1 \cdots c_k] = [m_1 \cdots m_k] + [g_1 \cdots g_h] \begin{bmatrix} b_{11}b_{12} \cdots b_{1k} \\ b_{21}b_{22} \cdots b_{2k} \\ \vdots \\ b_{h1}b_{h2} \cdots b_{hk} \end{bmatrix}$$

$$- [x_1 \cdots x_n] \begin{bmatrix} t_{11}t_{12} \cdots t_{1k} \\ t_{21}t_{22} \cdots t_{2k} \\ \vdots \\ t_{n1}t_{n2} \cdots t_{nk} \end{bmatrix} \qquad (3\text{-}2)$$

where

$\mathbf{c}$ = the post-fisc or final income vector, order $1 \times k$. An element, c_i, denotes the amount of income in income interval $i, i = 1, \ldots, k$;

$\mathbf{m}$ = the initial or factor income vector, order $1 \times k$;

$\mathbf{g}$ = a vector of government expenditures by category, order $1 \times h$;

$\mathbf{B}$ = a matrix of percentage distributors for government expenditures, order $h \times k$, whose rows each sum to one;

$\mathbf{x}$ = a vector of government tax receipts by category, order $1 \times n$;

$\mathbf{T}$ = a matrix of percentage distributors for government taxes, order $n \times k$, whose rows each sum to one.

Equations (3-1) and (3-2) reveal the simplicity of formulation for analysis of post-fisc distributions of income. Most of the empirical issues can be discussed in the order indicated by the right-hand side of (3-1) after the choice of post-war (World War II) years is explained.

Why 1950, 1961, and 1970?

Annual data on the post-fisc distribution of income over the entire post-World War II period, 1946–1975, would certainly be desirable, ceteris paribus. We could then produce a discussion comparable to that in the fine article by Budd (1970) on the distribution of money income in the United States since World War II. More information is generally preferred to less and data for only three years are clearly short of the ideal. Why have we settled for less?

The simple answer is that it would have been extremely costly to assemble and analyze reliable data for many additional years beyond these three. We searched for existing numbers which would be sufficient to compute the post-fisc distribution of equation (3-2). The equation is deceptive because, though simple, it makes enormous data demands, especially for the distributive matrices, $\mathbf{B}$ and $\mathbf{T}$.

Faced with such relative costs we chose to assemble a new data base for a recent year which could be made reasonably comparable with previous studies for earlier years. The logical choice was 1970 because a number of distributors were readily available from the Current Population Survey (Projector and Bretz 1972), and these could be supplemented with data from the *Statistics of Income 1970* (U.S. Department of Labor 1972) and miscellaneous sources in that year. A superior alternative would have been the *Survey of Consumer Expenditures, 1971–72* (BLS) but it was unavailable when this research began. The survey is conducted primarily to revise the weights in the Consumer Price Index but since it provides information on numerous expenditures and income sources by income class, it is a valuable base for distributive studies. In fact, the study for 1961 was based largely upon the *Survey of Consumer Expenditures, 1960–61* (BLS).

The years 1950 and 1961 were chosen because much of the relevant data had already been assembled in two previous studies by Conrad (1954) and the Tax Foundation (1967). A marriage of convenience need not always be infelicitous, and we believe that the three sets of data can and have been made as equivalent as analytically required. The influence of numerous differences among the procedures of the original studies has been mitigated by manipulations which approach a replication.

Our choice of three data points raises the issue of how representative these years are of the postwar era. Most analysts want to claim that their findings generalize to a much wider class of events. Of course, the extent to which the years 1950, 1961, and 1970 are representative can only be known by further empirical research within an ever widening set of conditions. At the least, these years are interesting for their own sake, especially because there were considerable changes in the size and composition of government during these two decades. While we do not *know* that our results generalize to the entire postwar era, we believe that the three years examined are representative of the postwar U.S. situation. The additional information which several more years would provide, while no doubt positive, would be small relative to the additional cost. Two reasons support this judgment. First, the evidence shows remarkably little variation in the overall distribution of money income in the United States since World War II (Budd 1970; Rivlin 1975). Second, year-to-year changes in aggregate government tax and expenditure policy are relatively small (Davis, Dempster, and Wildavsky 1966). However, the state of business activity can affect the size distribution of income (Metcalf 1972) as well as the composition of government receipts and expenditures (e.g., "automatic stabilizers") so we treat this issue in some detail at the end of the chapter.

The Income Aggregate

The pre-fisc distribution, **m,** has been obtained in practice by multiplying a probability distribution, which is the proportion of income in each income class, by a scalar which is always Net National Product in this study. A number of aggregate income bases have been used in the literature, possibly because each is appropriate for answering a particular question but also because little attention is generally given to this issue. In an intertemporal comparison, uniformity of definition is perhaps more important than finding the most appropriate aggregate income base, but nonetheless an income base must be selected. Our income base adds up to Net National Product (NNP). This seems appropriate because ultimately all claims to net output accrue to people; since we are dealing with all government taxes and expenditures, we should compare tax burdens and imputed expenditure gains with total output and hence total income by income group. Bishop (1966) and Meerman (1974) defend the use of Net National Product as an income base; but, for a contrary view, see McLure (1974). Of course, other income totals in a small neighborhood around NNP would have little effect on the distributive comparisons. NNP in current dollars was $265 billion in 1950, $474 billion in 1961, and $887 billion in 1970.

Many other studies of budget incidence begin with an aggregate of personal income before taxes and then add various imputed incomes by income class, such as realized capital gains, retained corporate earnings, income in kind from owner-occupied housing, home-grown food, and so forth. A prominent example has been the "broad income" concept of Gillespie (1965). The rationale for "broad income" lies in the answer to the question: What would be the distribution of earned income if there were no taxes? Thus broad income is an income concept derived from the zero government counterfactual. The question is answered as follows: Taxes shifted backward to factors would be received as factor income, but taxes shifted forward to consumers would not. Hence broad income consists of the backward shifted portion of taxes plus personal income before deduction of personal taxes minus personal transfer payments. A few other adjustments are made to get to factor returns not included in personal income. For example, undistributed corporate profits and realized capital gains are added.

The major quantitative difference between broad income and Net National Product is that the latter includes indirect business taxes. As Meerman (1974) has pointed out, a change from direct to indirect taxes which leaves the aggregate tax burden unaffected lowers broad income and makes tax burdens and expenditure benefits appear larger relative to initial income. Broad income does not seem appropriate for an intertemporal comparison in which uniformity is at a premium. (Perhaps it should be noted that income bases constructed by adding imputed incomes tend to be less unequally distributed than our factor income bases, although not very different from our money income base, which is also used.)

Income Intervals

More vexing than the somewhat arbitrary choice of total income is the construction of income classes, **m** in equation (3-1), which permits sensible comparisons over time. Ideally, of course, we would begin with error-free observations on individual income units. Instead, we begin with grouped data which are imperfect in a number of respects.[1] The income distribution data come from different sources and noncomparabilities arise which are not at all trivial. Major differences can be grouped under four headings. First, the objectives of the surveys differ and none has accurate measurement of the income distribution as the primary objective. For example, the Current Population Survey (CPS) is designed to measure attributes of the labor force while the BLS *Survey of Consumer Expenditures* is a detailed measure of expenditure patterns. Differences in objective can affect the numerical results because more detailed questioning will generally reveal more income and this can be disproportionately important at the extremes of the income distribution. Second, definitions of income receiving units as well as what comprises income differ from survey to survey. Third, the time periods to which the composition of the household and its income refer differ among surveys. Finally, sampling variability is a source of recorded differences.

Given these kinds of variation among sources of income data, careful description of procedures is warranted. The initial dollar intervals for income, the number of households, and the amount of income ascribed to each interval is determined by the official survey underlying the study for each year. Dollar intervals which define income classes remain unchanged throughout the analysis and households always remain in their initial bracket. This means that the initial distribution of households is never altered; households do not fall to lower intervals when taxes are subtracted from initial income nor do they rise when government expenditures are imputed to them.

Although the percentage distribution of households by income class is maintained in the vector of initial incomes (**m** in equation [3-1]), the income base is shifted from whatever aggregate income concept is implicit in the surveys to NNP. Since NNP exceeds aggregate income in the surveys, mean income within intervals often exceeds the upper bounds of the initial income brackets, but, to repeat, households remain grouped in their initial brackets.

The study for 1950 (Conrad 1954) was based upon the Federal Reserve System's *Survey of Consumer Finances* (SCF), which is still maintained by the Survey Research Center at the University of Michigan. The income receiving units were defined as "spending units," which basically means families and unrelated individuals who were not transients and were not in institutions. Income was defined to be wages and salaries, pensions and other transfers, interest and dividends, rents and earnings from farming,

---

[1] For extensive discussions of the problems with survey data on income, see National Bureau of Economic Research (1951), U.S. Bureau of the Budget (1966), U.S. Department of Labor Statistics (1971), and Cramer (1969, chap. 7).

unincorporated business, and professional practice.[2] The first five income intervals were in $1000 increments up to $5000, and the last two intervals are $5000–$7500 and over $7500. (The order of **m** in 1950 was 1 × 7.) The intervals were defined as income before personal taxes. See table C.1 for details.

The study for 1961 (Tax Foundation 1967) was based upon the BLS *Survey of Consumer Expenditures, 1960–61*. Since a different agency generated this set of data, with different objectives in mind, we should consider possible differences. The BLS data for 1961 has nine income intervals: under $2000, four $1000 increments up to $6000, $6000–$7500, $7500–$10,000, $10,000–$15,000 and over $15,000. (Thus, between 1950 and 1961, the order of **m** goes from 1 × 7 to 1 × 9.) The additional intervals are desirable, ceteris paribus, because they add information about the increased density of the distribution at incomes above $7500, reduce the bias toward underestimation of Gini ratios caused by fewer class intervals, and add degrees of freedom for the regression analyses that are undertaken. The data cover all noninstitutional consumer units, families and single consumers, excluding military personnel, and hence are virtually identical to the definition in the 1950 source. The definition of income is also comparable, except for one major complication. The published BLS distributions of income are *after* all personal taxes—federal, state, and local—are deducted. As might be expected, the dispersion in initial money income is thereby reduced because personal taxes are effectively progressive throughout much of the income range. The after-tax income base produces an incomparability relative to 1950 and 1970 which is large enough to warrant special attention. The data for 1961 were therefore adjusted, as described in the next section.

The 1970 distributions of income and households are based upon the Current Population Survey (CPS), as reported by Projector and Bretz (1972). This survey is very similar to BLS and SCF in its definition of income units and its definition of money income, but involved less detailed questioning about income. As a consequence, the CPS generally reports less income among low income units. For example, in 1961, CPS reported a larger percentage of families with incomes under $3000 than did BLS, but more seriously, the CPS reported that 32 percent of unrelated individuals had incomes under $1000 while the comparable figure reported by BLS was 16 percent. These are worrisome differences and the next section compares income dispersion as reported in various postwar surveys. Finally, a look at table C.3 (Appendix C) will show that the 1970 CPS reports eleven income intervals, with income defined before deduction of personal taxes: under

[2] See Conrad (1954, pp. 184–85) for further references.

$2000, six $1000 increments to $8000, $8000 to $10,000, $10,000 to $15,000, $15,000 to $25,000, and over $25,000. (The order of **m** has now become 1 × 11.)

Adjusting Income Intervals for 1961

A glance at equation (3-1) shows that the initial distribution of income, denoted by **m**, is a determinant of the post-fisc distribution, **c**. The use of income intervals after the deduction of personal taxes in the 1961 study creates a potential downward bias in the pre-fisc and hence in the post-fisc distribution of income, relative to 1950 and 1970. To begin an analysis of this problem, table 3.1 shows distributions of households by income brackets, as reported by various sources for 1959 and 1961. There are rather obvious differences between surveys in the proportion of households

TABLE 3.1

Comparison of Distribution of Households by Income, Various Sources, 1959 and 1961

Income Brackets	All Families and Individuals					
	1959 Decennial Census	1961 Unpublished BLS	1961 Published BLS[a]	1961 CPS	1961 OBE	1961 Michigan SCF
Percentage distribution, total	100.0	100.0	100.0	100.0	100.0	100.0
Under $2000	23.3	13.5	14.2	20.9	12.9	18.0
$2000–$2999	9.2	10.0	11.0	9.4	9.1	10.0
$3000–$3999	9.5	10.3	11.5	9.6	10.3	10.0
$4000–$4999	10.2	10.8	12.6	10.0	10.8	11.0
$5000–$5999	10.7	11.4	12.7	10.6	10.5	12.0
$6000–$7499	} 25.1	14.3	15.2	} 26.1	14.1	14.0
$7500–$9999		15.6	13.7		14.7	12.0
$10,000–$14,999	} 12.0	10.4	7.2	9.4	11.1	9.0
$15,000 and over		3.7	2.0	4.0	6.5	4.0
Mean	$5696	$6246	$6294	$5896	$6930	$6050
Median	$4791	—	—	$5009	—	$5000

SOURCES: For comparison of 1959 Decennial Census, 1961 unpublished BLS, 1961 CPS, and 1961 OBE, see U.S. Department of Labor (1971, p. 53). Also see p. 53 for original sources. For 1961 published BLS, see Tax Foundation (1967, p. 47). For 1961 Michigan SCF, see Survey Research Center (1963).

[a] The income brackets are as defined by each agency. In all cases, the income brackets are before deduction of personal taxes *except* for the 1961 published BLS data, which are income after deduction of personal taxes.

in various income brackets, especially at the tails of the distributions. For instance, the 1959 Decennial Census reports 23 percent of households below $2000 while the 1961 OBE (Office of Business Economics, Department of Commerce) reports 13 percent.

The prime object of interest is the third distribution in table 3.1, the 1961 published BLS. Relative to the other distributions, it has a relatively small proportion of units under $2000 but it also has the fewest above $10,000. The more compact distribution reflects two characteristics of the BLS distribution: the first is that more detailed questioning about income sources raises income generally, and, second, deduction of personal taxes disproportionately reduces high incomes.

Before deciding how to handle this problem, it is useful to consider a more complete comparison of income distributions from various sources for the postwar period. The Gini concentration ratio is the most popular summary statistic for comparing income distributions, and table 3.2 reports a large number of these ratios. They provide further background for evaluating the suitability of the BLS as the 1961 factor income base. As the row means indicate, CPS and OBE Gini ratios average about .420 while IRS Gini ratios average about .440. (This difference is partly due to the exclusion of government transfers from personal income taxation, and hence from the IRS data.) Gini ratios calculated from the Michigan SCF are somewhat lower, about .400. The mean of the BLS concentration ratios is considerably lower than all the others, standing at about .340. Obviously the BLS income base, as reported in the original study for 1961 (Tax Foundation 1967), cannot be considered comparable to the income bases used for 1950 (SCF) and 1970 (CPS). By virtually any comparison within table 3.2, the 1961 BLS income dispersion appears suspiciously small.

As a remedy for the low dispersion of the 1961 BLS distribution we have substituted the Michigan SCF distribution of households and income for 1961. This appears to be a sensible substitution for a couple of reasons. First, the SCF was the basis for the 1950 study (Conrad 1954) and its use in 1961 continues this practice. Second, the Michigan SCF Gini, .398, preserves the same order of magnitude for pre-fisc dispersion in money income as for the 1950 SCF and 1970 CPS. This is desirable because there is no reason to believe that overall Gini ratios are very different during this period. Note that the Gini ratios for money income are lower than the Gini coefficients for all IRS returns for the corresponding year.

The CPS might have been used instead of the Michigan SCF distribution of households because they are quite close in table 3.1. Both the Michigan SCF and CPS for 1961 perhaps have too many households below $2000, but the Michigan SCF is less extreme in this respect. Either choice is superior to the published BLS for 1961, but the Michigan SCF is our choice.

TABLE 3.2

Gini Concentration Ratios from Various Sources, Selected Years, 1950–1973

Source	1950	1955	1958	1960	1961	1965	1967	1970	1973	Row Mean
CPS										
1. Budd	.431	.420	.416	.423	.432	.417	.416	—	—	.422
2. Schultz	.424	.451	.402	.415	.427	.414	—	—	—	.422
3. Danziger	.415	.415	.405	.415	.424	.408	.404	.409	.416	.412
IRS										
4. Budd	.425	.435	—	.443	—	—	.468	—	—	.443
5. Gastwirth	—	.426	.431	.434	.441	.450	.457	—	—	.440
6. Danziger	.432	.434	.438	.442	.446	.458	.465	.453	—	.446
7. *OBE*	.423	—	—	.415	.417	—	—	.402	—	.414
8. *BLS*	.330	—	—	.338	.362	—	—	—	—	.343
9. *HENLE*	—	—	.399	.411	.420	—	.412	.420	—	.412
10. *MICHIGAN SCF*	.391	.411	.382	.372	.398	.388	.379	.380	—	.388
11. *R-S*										
Money	.391	—	—	—	.398	—	—	.400	—	.396
Money minus transfers	.408	—	—	—	.433	—	—	.452	—	.434
Factor	.436	—	—	—	.436	—	—	.446	—	.439
Column mean	.410				.418			.426		

SOURCES:
1. Budd (1970).
2. Schultz (1969).
3. Danziger and Smolensky (1975).
4. Budd (1970).
5 Gastwirth (1972).
6. Danziger and Smolensky (1975).
7. U.S. Department of Labor (1971), as quoted in Budd (1970) and Radner and Hinrichs (1974).
8. Calculated from U.S. Department of Labor (1971), as quoted in Budd (1970) and Reynolds and Smolensky (1974).
9. Henle (1972).
10. Calculated from Survey Research Center (1961, 1963, 1969, and 1973).
11. Calculated from data in Appendixes C and E.

Choice of an initial distribution of households by income bracket is very important, but its importance is mitigated somewhat by the fact that the empirical work in chapters 4 and 5 is based upon two alternative initial distributions. The first is the SCF distributions of money income in 1950 and 1961 and the CPS distribution for 1970. These distributions appear to have Gini ratios which are somewhat below the average shown in table 3.2. However, our primary pre-fisc income distribution will be the factor income base, explained in a subsequent section and in Appendix C. The Gini ratios for this income base are .436 in 1950, .436 in 1961, and .446 in 1970. These Gini ratios are somewhat higher than most of those in table 3.2, and approximate the large Gini ratios for IRS returns. Two income bases appear to meet potential objections based upon the special nature of any single income base. Factor income is constructed using distributors from Appendix B and we should note that all the BLS distributors for 1961 have been adjusted (scaled upward) by the Michigan distribution of households. The adjustment procedure is explained in the section on the distributive matrix below.

Two Income Distributions

Appendix C describes the two pre-fisc income bases constructed for each year. In the first income base, NNP is simply distributed across income classes as money income was in that year. We refer to this as "the money income base." This distribution is comparable to those used in some earlier studies, and it has been retained because our concern is an intertemporal comparison.

A major criticism, however, is that this income distribution already includes the consequences of government cash transfers. Initial income dispersion is smaller than the dispersion in factor earnings as a result. Since government transfers will be distributed across income classes in subsequent calculations, it could well be argued that the degree of dispersion in the post-fisc distributions is biased downward. Since cash transfers have been growing rapidly, the bias is potentially larger in later years. One solution to this problem is to construct an alternative income base that distributes NNP as factor earnings were distributed in that year. Such an income base has been created for each of the three years and is referred to as the "factor income base." To construct this base the dollar amounts of the five major types of factor earnings—employee compensation, proprietor income, rent, interest, and corporate profits—plus indirect business taxes were imputed to households by income class, using appropriate distributors from Appendix B. A percentage distribution was then formed and applied to NNP. Relative to the distribution of money income, the share of factor earnings is slightly smaller in all income classes but the highest. This difference is due primarily to corporate profits, which are distributed by share of dividend income; the highest income class realizes a large share. For example, the Gini coefficient for factor NNP in 1970 is .446 and for money NNP is .400.

In terms of income dispersion, factor income is close to money income minus cash transfers from government. If cash transfers are defined to include only Social Security benefits, public assistance, unemployment compensation, and other transfers, the Gini ratios for money income minus transfers are .408, .433, and .452 in 1950, 1961, and 1970, respectively. The Gini ratios for factor income are .436, .436, and .446, respectively. The only puzzling result is the very small rise in the 1950 Gini ratio for money income from .391 to .408 after deduction of government cash transfers. The explanation is that cash transfers by government were very small in 1950.[3]

Measuring Burdens and Benefits

Proceeding from equation (3-1) the next problem is to calculate taxes, vector **x**, and expenditures, vector **g**, in monetary terms. The amounts allocated to households on the tax and expenditure sides are total government receipts and expenditures as reported in the national income accounts, *Survey of Current Business,* annually in the July issue. This obviously simplifies the problem enormously and also has the virtue of consistency with the NNP income base from the national income accounts. We include all levels of government which means that, in an accounting sense, state–local receipts and expenditures are distributionally indistinguishable from those made by the central government. Nontax payments in the form of license fees and user charges levied by state and local governments, which amounted to 13 percent of state–local receipts in 1970, are counted as taxes, which means that the difference between all government receipts and expenditures is limited to the total federal–state–local surplus or deficit in the national income accounts. The total surplus was $3.6 billion in 1950 or 1.4 percent of NNP, and total deficits were $4.3 billion in 1961 or 0.9 percent of NNP and $13.1 billion in 1970 or 1.5 percent of NNP. Symbolically,

$$\sum_{i=1}^{h} g_i \cong \sum_{j=1}^{n} x_j, \qquad (3\text{-}3)$$

[3] Table 3.2 offers an extensive comparison of postwar Gini ratios. The Gini coefficient for "original income" minus transfers in the Conrad (1954) study was .447 because transfers were more broadly defined. They included veterans' payments, interest paid by government, and agricultural subsidies. Original income minus transfers was the basic distributor used to generate the factor income base for 1950, because the specific distributors used for 1961 and 1970 were not available for 1950. The exact procedures are detailed in Appendix C. If, instead of distributing NNP by factor or money income to obtain the initial income distributions, definitions of roughly comparable aggregates from the National Income Accounts had been used, the quantitative differences would have been small, even in any one year. Thus, using the Office of Business Economics definitions, the Gini coefficients on NNP and National Income were .433 and .443, respectively, in 1970. This compares with .446 for the factor income base. The Gini coefficient for Personal Income in 1970 was .385; for the money income base .400. To reiterate, however, consistency over time is probably more important than the definition in any one year.

that is, government expenditures approximately equal government tax receipts and hence, because $\sum g - \sum x = 0$ it follows that

$$\sum_{}^{k} c = \sum_{}^{k} m = \text{NNP}. \tag{3-4}$$

While our measurement procedure is straightforward, it raises a number of questions which are common enough when numbers generated by accountants for special purposes are used by economists for entirely different purposes. Conceptually we wish to measure the tax "burden," which means the amount of market income sacrificed (goods and services), in total, by the community in favor of government activity. Tax receipts seem to be accepted as a reasonably satisfactory measure of the current resource costs of government activity, if we can judge by the silence in the literature. However, it is accurate to say that tax receipts ignore any indirect costs associated with the level and composition of taxes. In addition, various tax subsidies, market regulations, and other implicit taxes (such as unanticipated inflation, military conscription, and compulsory schooling) which are small in explicit budget accounts but potentially large in distributive effects are not taken into account. There is no natural way to account for them but it is also fair to note that, if these other factors are similar across years, the analysis remains an unbiased estimate of change over time.

The expenditure side appears more controversial. Expenditures by government affect the income distribution two ways: one is through the expenditures per se, and the other is through the output of goods and services associated with those expenditures. Expenditures are made to purchase goods and services, and obviously are income to the suppliers of those goods and services. A second kind of expenditure by government is cash transferred to households for which government receives no current direct goods and services in return. This money flow is not synonymous with the flow or distribution of the benefits of public outputs to households. This flow of government benefits, valued at their current monetary cost to government, is what is measured in this study and divided among income classes in an analogous manner to that for taxes. The distribution of benefits coincides with the distribution of expenditures in the case of cash transfers only. The distribution of the benefits of government output rather than the flow of payments is what is allocated by income class because we assume that government is a pricetaker in factor markets. Payments to civil servants, defense contractors, and highway contractors are assumed to just cover their opportunity costs. A somewhat weaker assumption that is sufficient is that any excess paid to suppliers because government is a less efficient buyer than private firms or any savings due to say economies of scale in purchasing are errors of a constant proportion of the government budget.

The procedure can obviously be criticized on a number of grounds, and enumerating them may help in interpreting the results. For instance, assuming that government services can be valued at their current cost implies a government of model virtue in terms of production efficiency, which is not realized in practice but for which there is no obvious way to rescale. Once again, any errors are assumed similar by year. On a narrower point, current monetary expenditures may not match the current value flowing from capital-intensive goods like highways, flows which also emanate from large capital investments in the past. Government capital investments are assumed to be a stable item over time. (Since we allocate NNP and not Gross National Product [GNP], a similar criticism applies to the private sector.) In a highly aggregate study, little would be gained by an elaborate allocation of capital accounts over time.

This raises some more general problems with our treatment of expenditure benefits. Interest payments, veterans' benefits, and government pensions are treated as simple cash transfers from taxpayers to the recipients. Each of these categories, but especially interest paid, can be considered a factor cost for the production of government services rather than a transfer program. Government interest payments are no different from servicing private debt, and such outlays represent the premium government must pay for the use of resources in the past or present in excess of tax receipts. Another limitation is that some expenditures may be small in the budget but the associated output may be highly valued, say, the legal system. In such cases, expenditures may understate benefits by income class but an efficiency argument can rationalize this treatment. If government were efficient in all activities, each activity would be produced in an amount such that the cost of providing an additional unit just equaled the marginal valuation in the community. Under the usual accounting convention, this would be valued at total expenditures, not some procedure involving consumers' surplus. Of course no accounting of consumer surplus is made for the private sector either. Similarly, there is no attempt to account for external and/or indirect effects among expenditure programs. For example, cash and in-kind transfers have been assumed to increase the income of direct recipients by the amount of the expenditure and to decrease incomes of taxpayers, with no accounting for indirect benefits or costs to nonrecipients.

The Distributors

Assigning burdens and benefits by income class demands numbers for the distributive matrices denoted by **B** and **T** in equation (3-2). A rich variety of distributors, hopefully with little observation error, is desirable to reflect the numerous assumptions about incidence which are possible for the many taxes and expenditures. In addition, of course, it would be nice to have equivalent distributors, by type and quality, for each year.

There are numerous difficulties in achieving parity among distributors for each year. Exact details are reported in Appendix B but major problems and their resolution can be discussed here. The 1950 distributors are entirely from Conrad (1954), except for the addition of a distributor for higher education and for primary–secondary education which would be comparable to the distributors for 1961 and 1970 (cf. items 18 and 19 in table B.1). These distributors are somewhat more concentrated in upper income classes, as measured by the Gini concentration ratio, than the distributors for 1961 and 1970. This may reflect real changes in the world during this period but, even if it does not, relatively small expenditures on education are involved in 1950 and distributive results would be insensitive to somewhat different distributors. Other discrepancies between the 1950 distributors and their counterparts for 1961 and 1970 are even less serious. We might note, however, that Conrad (1954) originally assembled his set of distributors from a scattered series of sources of unknown quality.

The 1961 distributors are all derived from the Tax Foundation (1967) except for the substitution of the Michigan SCF distribution of households and money income, items 1 and 2 in table B.2, plus the addition of a distributor for rental income from the *Statistics of Income, 1961* (U.S. Department of the Treasury 1964), item 7 in table B.2. The primary source for the distributive matrix was, of course, the BLS *Survey of Consumer Expenditures,* which probably excels in thoroughness, consistency, and homogeneity among the three years. A major deficiency of these distributors, however, is that the income intervals were reported as money income after deduction of all personal taxes. To correct this problem, all BLS distributors have been rescaled upward to conform to the Michigan SCF distribution of initial income. The basic assumption in the adjustment procedure is that only the households near the brackets are affected by the pre- versus posttax income intervals. This assumption simplifies matters considerably because it implies that the expenditures of these "borderline" households are similar enough so that only the relative change in the number of households that move between two intervals affect the values of distributors. In other words, if some income interval has a smaller proportion of households in the Michigan SCF than in the BLS survey, expenditure proportions are reduced accordingly. The precise rescaling can be stated as:

$$A_{ij} = \frac{(f_{Mj}/f_{Bj})e_{ij}}{\sum_{j=1}^{9}[(f_{Mj}/f_{Bj})e_{ij}]} \tag{3-5}$$

where

A_{ij} = the percentage of expenditure item i in income class j,
f_{Mj} = the percentage of Michigan SCF households in income class j,

f_{Bj} = the percentage of BLS households in income class j,
e_{ij} = the percentage of BLS expenditure item i in income class j.

The denominator in equation (3-5) is required because row totals do not generally equal 100 percent, so each entry is divided by its corresponding row total.

The 1970 matrix is assembled from a variety of sources, as was the original 1950 matrix, and probably suffers (unknown) defects as a consequence. The two major sources are the CPS (Projector and Bretz 1972) and the *Statistics of Income 1970* (U.S. Department of the Treasury 1972). Miscellaneous sources for other distributors, items 14–19 in table B.3, are documented in Appendix footnotes. Curiously, we might note that Gini ratios for dividends, interest income, farm income, personal income tax, housing, auto, and education expenditures are lowest in 1970. Although we do not know what kinds of measurement error may exist, the numerical results are certainly affected by the degree of concentration in various distributors. For example, if the distribution of interest income is closer to equality in 1970 than in 1950 and it is used to distribute expenditures on net interest, these expenditures will be less disequalizing in 1970 than they were in 1950. The net effect of multiple distributive changes is difficult to assess without some formal aggregation procedure.

Some oddities to note about the 1970 distributors are the reliance on some IRS data, which are especially defective in terms of the definition of income receiving unit (returns), and the use of mean house value of owners, as reported in the Michigan SCF, for item 16 in table B.3 instead of housing expenditures by renters and owners. Consumption expenditures and higher education expenditures are estimated from 1961 data.

Although the final judgment must rest with our critics, we believe that the distributive matrices are relatively comparable across years. Inevitably a series of compromises are made during an extended study of this kind. Perhaps the most serious questions concern the nature and degree of observational error in the data, but we simply do not know the answers to these questions with any positive degree of confidence. We suspect that our numbers generally mirror real phenomena but any serious defense would hardly be convincing, especially when presented by the consumers rather than the producers of the data.

The Business Cycle

An important restriction on any secular interpretation of distributive changes among the years 1950, 1961, and 1970 is the cyclical nature of business activity. Since business fluctuations can affect dispersion in money income, any differences among these three years might simply be transitory differences with no secular component. To assess the possibility, consider the chronology of business cycles according to the National Bureau of Economic Research (1973). The NBER characterized 1950 as a revival year. The trough was in November 1949, and the subsequent peak was reached during the fourth quarter of 1953. The year 1961 was also a revival year, by and large, for the nearest trough has been set at February of that year. The unusually long upswing, which began in 1961, terminated during the first quarter of 1970 and was resumed in December of that year. Both a peak and a trough were experienced in that year, but it was mainly a year of very modest recession. (Nominal GNP rose nearly 7 percent from the first to the fourth quarter.)

One way to portray the significance of the cycle for this study appears as figure 3.1. The shaded areas represent the short cycles around the three years of this study. Two annual time series of Gini coefficients also appear

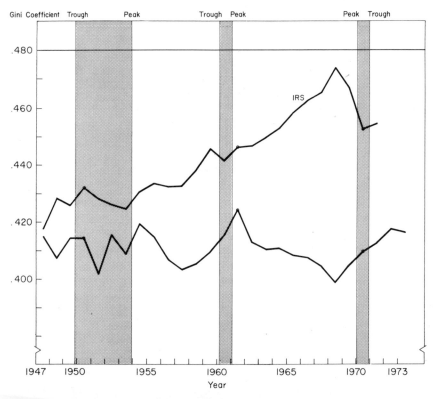

FIGURE 3.1 *Time series of the IRS and CPS Gini coefficient and the NBER reference cycles, 1947–1973. [Sources: Danziger and Smolensky 1975, and National Bureau of Economic Research 1973.]*

TABLE 3.3
Selected Expenditures and Taxes as a Percentage of NNP, Selected Years

Category	1949	1950	1951	1960	1961	1962	1969	1970	1971
Total federal expenditures	17.2	15.3	18.8	20.2	21.5	21.6	22.3	22.9	23.0
Federal transfers	5.8	5.4	3.8	5.1	5.7	5.4	6.2	7.1	7.8
Total state and local expenditures	8.4	8.4	7.7	10.8	11.4	11.3	14.0	15.0	15.4
Total state and local transfers	1.2	1.3	1.0	1.1	1.2	1.1	1.4	1.6	1.7
Corporate tax									
Federal	4.1	6.4	7.0	4.7	4.6	4.5	4.3	3.5	3.5
State and local	.3	.3	.3	.3	.3	.3	.4	.4	.4

SOURCES: U.S. Department of Commerce, *The National Income and Product Accounts of the United States, 1929–1965: Statistical Tables,* tables 1.9, 3.1, and 3.3, and the same tables in *Survey of Current Business* 53 (July 1973).

in the figure. The CPS series is quite close to the concept of money income used in this study. The IRS series excludes cash transfers and is similar to our concept of factor income. The years 1950 and 1961 are local maxima in both series, as would be expected at the lower turning points of the cycle (Metcalf 1972). For the year 1970, a short interlude in an expansion, the CPS Gini is neither a local maximum nor a local minimum. The IRS Gini for 1970 lags the peak by a year.

Figure 3.1 shows that 1950, 1961, and 1970 were at rather similar stages in the business cycle. All are reasonably near a cyclical trough, although technically 1961 contains a peak. This is a fortuitous event. However, 1970 may be the least similar, especially since local maxima in Gini coefficients occurred in 1950 and 1961 but not in 1970. The CPS series shows a local maximum in 1972 and the IRS series peaks in 1968. But the substitution of one of these years for 1970 is surely not justified on the basis of such differences.

The business cycle can be expected to affect the level and composition of government expenditures and taxes and hence the fact that our three years are at somewhat different stages of the cycle might be expected to affect the post-fisc distribution in ways other than through the initial distribution. In table 3.3, several indicators of such potential effects are shown. It is apparent from the table that cyclical effects are quite small relative to trend. There is a surprising cyclically reinforcing decline in the ratio of federal expenditures and transfers to NNP in 1950, which may bias the post-fisc 1950 Gini coefficient upward.

4
Empirical Results

Economics needs induction and deduction, but in different proportions to different purposes. [Alfred Marshall 1948, p. *xix*]

There is little consensus concerning the best way to describe a size distribution of income, much less on how best to contrast many distributions.[1] For this reason a variety of analytical and graphical techniques will be used in this chapter and the next to compare the post-fisc distributions we have constructed for 1950, 1961, and 1970.

Just as there is no unanimity on the best measure of dispersion, so there is no consensus on the incidence of several taxes and expenditures. A number of different incidence assumptions are therefore employed, which considerably expands the number of comparisons. Some conclusions emerge out of this welter of comparisons which are robust enough to survive under all the combinations of technique and incidence assumptions.

The usual device in studies of budget incidence is to report a bewildering mass of tax and expenditure ratios by income class. Although such ratios are presented in this chapter and in Appendixes D and E, in this chapter, we primarily use simple linear regressions to summarize and compare distributions by years. First, however, we consider how changes in government budgets since 1950 might have affected post-fisc distributions. Next, the bases for allocating taxes and expenditures are described. Finally, the empirical results of the linear regression model are discussed under five alternative sets of incidence assumptions.

A Set of Expectations

The National Income Accounts reveal some relevant trends between 1950 and 1970. Nominal Net National Product (NNP) has grown from $265

[1] For informative discussions about measuring dispersion, see Lydall (1968, pp. 137–41); Stark (1972, pp. 137–53); Champernowne (1974, pp. 787–816); Wiles (1974, pp. ix–xii); and Sen (1973, pp. 24–46).

billion in 1950 to $887 billion in 1970, an increase in each decade of about 80 percent. During these years, as the Appendixes indicate, government has grown much faster, raising the ratio of government spending at all levels to NNP from 20 percent in 1950 to 31 percent in 1961 and to more than 35 percent in 1970. From a purely accounting point of view, the growth of the government share is a factor that, ceteris paribus, reduces inequality in the after-tax, after-expenditure pattern of distribution because public output is more equally distributed than private output.[2]

Estimated post-fisc distributions are affected not only by the size of the government relative to NNP but also by its composition. First, consider the composition of taxes. Total state and local taxes have risen from 42 percent of total federal taxes in 1950 to 51 percent in 1961 to 58 percent in 1970. This would imply a gradual decline in the degree of progressivity of the overall tax structure because state and local tax structures are generally believed to be less progressive than the federal tax structure.[3] Among state and local taxes, the personal income tax and sales taxes, excises, and fees have grown most rapidly, with each type of tax raising its relative share in tax receipts by five percentage points. The relative decline has occurred in the property tax, which fell from 43 percent of all state and local tax receipts in 1950 to 33 percent in 1970. This would commonly be interpreted as indicating a decline in the degree of regressivity in the average state–local tax structure because property taxes are often viewed as the most regressive tax with respect to current income. Obviously, however, this interpretation is very sensitive to the assumed incidence pattern for each kind of tax.

The structure of the federal tax totals has changed more dramatically than the national tax totals for state and local governments. The corporate income tax has gradually declined from 27 percent of federal tax receipts in 1950 to 16 percent in 1970. Similarly, excise and customs taxes have declined from 20 percent in 1950 to 10 percent in 1970. Social Security payroll taxes have grown much more rapidly than all federal taxes, increasing their share from less than 9 percent in 1950 to 26 percent in 1970. Receipts from the personal income tax have grown slightly faster than all federal taxes, increasing their share by four percentage points to 46 percent. Although a judgment about the net change in the degree of progressivity in the federal tax structure depends upon incidence assumptions, these changes appear to decrease progressivity. The large changes are declining corporate

---

[2] If income originating in the government sector also were more equally distributed than income originating in the private sector, even greater equality in the pretax, pretransfer distributions would result, ceteris paribus.

[3] For present purposes, progressivity is defined with respect to current income rather than an alternative like permanent income, or proxy measures for it, like house values or consumption expenditures.

income taxes and growing payroll taxes; these are generally regarded as regressive changes unless the corporate tax is believed to fall almost exclusively upon consumers. The relative decline of federal excise receipts and the relative increase in personal income taxes can be viewed as largely offsetting each other. According to these arguments, it appears that the federal tax structure became less progressive over time while state and local governments, on average, became less regressive.

It is somewhat more difficult to generate expectations about the distributive effects of expenditures because of the relatively recent development of incidence assumptions for various types of expenditures. First, consider the relative size of state–local expenditures compared to federal expenditures. State–local expenditures have increased much more rapidly than have federal expenditures, rising from 38 percent of federal expenditures in 1950 to 52 percent in 1961 to 74 percent in 1970.[4] This change in the composition of government expenditures could affect the distributional impact of government, but there is no consensus about whether federal or state–local governments are more progressive in expenditures.[5]

Among federal expenditures, there have been sizable declines between 1950 and 1970 in the share of the budget used for veterans' benefits, interest paid, and agriculture. The budget shares increased in each of three primary areas: national defense, other "indivisible" government expenditures, and, most dramatically, Social Security expenditures; the latter grew from less than 6 percent of the federal budget in 1950 to 23 percent in 1970. If allocated across income classes in a conventional manner, these shifts in the structure of federal outlays are increasingly pro-poor. The only major budget changes in aggregate state and local outlays are a sharp growth in the share of educational expenditures, from 24 percent in 1950 to 41 percent in 1970, and a reduction in the share for streets and highways from more than 21 percent in 1950 to less than 12 percent in 1970. Somewhat surprisingly, public assistance and similar transfer programs are not allotted a higher share of state–local budgets in 1970 than in 1950 and 1961. Other compositional changes at the state and local level are difficult to assess, but it appears likely that expenditure patterns are more pro-poor in later years.

[4] Put in different terms, state–local expenditures have arisen from 5.6 percent of NNP in 1950 to 15.0 percent in 1970, while federal expenditures have risen more slowly from 14.6 percent of NNP in 1950 to 20.4 percent in 1970. Note, however, that $24 billion of state–local expenditures financed by federal grants-in-aid for 1970 appear in state and local expenditures, not in federal expenditures.

[5] Gillespie (1965, pp. 164–65) finds state–local government more pro-poor in expenditure incidence than the federal government and the Tax Foundation (1967) does not explicitly make an expenditure comparison between levels of government, although taxes are compared. Since grants-in-aid and many other factors undoubtedly alter state expenditure and tax schedules, it may not be meaningful to arithmetically separate the effects of levels of government.

On balance, the combined distributive impact of all levels of government upon the distribution of final income cannot be confidently predicted from these factors. Most of the changes in the size and composition of governments, however, appear to be increasingly pro-poor. Only the expansion of state–local governments relative to the federal government and the apparently lower progressivity of the federal tax structure are factors reducing the pro-poor direction of the fisc, at least in an accounting sense.

Standard Incidence Assumptions

The discovery of who bears the burden of particular taxes has proven very elusive to some of the best talent in the economics profession over the years. Theoretical results about the incidence of taxes remain very sensitive to the assumed form of the model, with implications turning on issues such as the elasticities of aggregate supplies of factor inputs or the time period of adjustment in a general equilibrium system. Empirical verification has been no more successful in eliminating differences of opinion. The unresolved debate over the degree of shifting in the corporate income tax is a classic illustration (Krzyzaniak and Musgrave 1963; Cragg, Harberger, and Mieszkowski 1967; and Gordon 1967). However, there has been a recent evolution of views toward the position that taxes on corporate income and property are borne in proportion to the ownership of nonhuman capital in general. This conclusion derives from the following kind of reasoning: the corporate income tax depresses rates of return in the corporate sector when it is imposed, but this encourages investment in the noncorporate sector. As the supply of capital in the noncorporate sector increases, rates of return decline until net returns after tax are the same in all sectors. Thus, if total investment in the economy is perfectly inelastic, a tax on returns to capital ownership in one sector ultimately depresses the posttax rate of return to all forms of capital ownership.

In the absence of a theoretical and empirical consensus about incidence in taxes, as well as the incidence of expenditure benefits, we have followed in the pragmatic footsteps of other analysts who have tried to estimate the distribution of after-tax and after-expenditure income. We have adopted a relatively conventional set of incidence assumptions in our standard case and also present calculations with three alternative sets of assumptions. The purpose is to discover how sensitive results are to combinations of incidence assumptions. The emphasis upon using a "correct" set of assumptions is greatly reduced by examining the effects of alternatives, but the issue is further deemphasized by our attention to systematic comparisons over time. In other words, the empirical results in a single year are extremely sensitive to incidence assumptions but, if common incidence assumptions are adopted for each year, the same intertemporal changes might well recur under all sets of incidence assumptions. In such cases, incidence assumptions no longer make a crucial difference to empirical results and our ignorance about incidence need not prohibit drawing inferences about the course of post-fisc distributions since 1950.

Table 4.1 summarizes the bases for allocating taxes and expenditures in the standard case. We have called it "standard" because the incidence assumptions are the conventional, intermediate assumptions of previous studies, especially those for 1961 and 1970. Incidence is intermediate in the sense that more regressive or progressive assumptions are plausible. The key assumptions are: personal income taxes are not shifted, estate and gift taxes are paid by the highest income class, the corporate income tax is divided equally between dividend recipients and consumers, excise and sales taxes are borne entirely by consumers, Social Security payroll taxes are borne entirely by employees, and the property tax is paid by consumers of housing in the residential sector and consumers of general output for commercial property taxes. The incidence of expenditures is assumed to fall entirely on recipients rather directly identified as beneficiaries—for example, automobile owners for highway expenditures or children under 18 for elementary and secondary expenditures. The general expenditures of government for

TABLE 4.1

Standard Incidence Assumptions

Category	Distributor by Income Class[a]
Tax	
Personal income tax	Personal income tax
Estate and gift tax	Highest income class
Corporate income tax	$\frac{1}{2}$ dividends, $\frac{1}{2}$ consumption
Sales, excise, and customs taxes	Consumption
Property tax	$\frac{1}{2}$ housing expenditures, $\frac{1}{2}$ consumption
Social Security tax	Employee payroll tax
Expenditure	
General expenditures	$\frac{1}{2}$ households, $\frac{1}{2}$ income
Cash transfers	Respective distributors for cash transfers
Interest	Interest income
Agriculture	Farm income
Elementary and secondary education	Children under 18
Higher education	Expenditures on higher education
Highways	Automobiles owned
Labor	Wages and salaries

[a] Distributors by income class are presented in Appendix B. Precise definitions, which may vary slightly, and sources are described in the notes to Appendix B.

which direct beneficiaries cannot be readily identified are arbitrarily distributed, one-half by the distribution of households and one-half by share of initial income. The rationale is that households benefit on some equalitarian basis as well as in proportion to income. General expenditures are about one-half of federal and one-third of state and local outlays.

There are only minor discrepancies across years in the type of distributor used to allocate particular taxes and expenditures in the standard case. Among taxes, the only discrepancy is the retention of particular excise and sales tax distributors developed in the 1950 and 1961 studies, and the use of general consumption in 1970. However, the Gini ratios for these distributors are all very close and it makes little practical difference. For example, the Gini ratio for the distributor of excise and customs in 1950 is .341. In 1961, excise and customs is allocated by a host of distributors which in the aggregate have a Gini of .320. For 1970, the distributor is general consumption which has a Gini of .338. Among expenditures, the only difference worth mentioning is that 1961 highway expenditures are distributed one-half by general consumption and one-half by auto expenditures, while these expenditures are exclusively distributed by auto expenditures in 1950 and 1970. The rationale for 1961 was that a portion of highway benefits accrues through reduction of product prices due to lower commercial transport costs. We retain this assumption for 1961 although general consumption is somewhat more skewed toward the extreme classes than auto expenditures. For further detail on all tax and expenditure distributors see footnotes to Appendixes D and E.

Taxes and Expenditures as a Percentage of Income

The most common technique for presenting the results of budget incidence studies is to describe the ratios of taxes and expenditures to income within income classes and to then assess the overall pattern across income classes. Following this tradition, table 4.2 presents ratios of total benefits from expenditures received or total taxes paid in an income class to the factor income in that same class. Expenditures are totals for all levels of government using standard incidence assumptions (details in Appendix E). The factor income base is described in detail in Appendix C. Recall that the dollar amount of income in each class is unaffected when alternative incidence assumptions are employed. The total amounts of taxes, under standard incidence assumptions, are obtained from Appendix D.

Taxes as a fraction of' factor income trace a roughly similar pattern across the income classes in all three years. The fraction is largest in the lowest income class in two of the years and second largest in the third year.

TABLE 4.2

Expenditures and Taxes as a Percentage of Factor Income, Standard Incidence, 1950, 1961, and 1970

Income Class	$\left(\dfrac{\text{Taxes}}{\text{Factor Income}}\right) \times 100$			$\left(\dfrac{\text{Expenditures}}{\text{Factor Income}}\right) \times 100$		
	1950	1961	1970	1950	1961	1970
$0–1000	29.1	} 38.6	} 58.8	160.9	} 179.6	} 315.7
1000–2000	16.4			35.3		
2000–3000	19.4	30.7	45.9	23.6	85.7	173.7
3000–4000	20.5	29.7	44.7	19.8	52.8	118.4
4000–5000	20.0	28.9	41.4	16.1	36.4	85.5
5000–6000		28.4	38.5		31.1	60.9
6000–7000	} 18.5	} 28.3	36.2	} 14.7	} 27.3	48.4
7000–7500			} 34.4			} 41.0
7500–8000		} 27.9			} 23.4	
8000–10,000			34.0			35.8
10,000–15,000	} 28.0	28.7	31.2	} 10.9	20.8	29.4
15,000–25,000		} 39.0	29.2		} 17.5	22.7
25,000+			39.7			17.2
Total	21.6	30.5	33.9	20.3	31.4	35.4

SOURCES: Appendixes C–E.

The ratio is second largest in the uppermost income class in two years and highest in the third year. This U-shaped pattern, particularly the high ratio in the lowest income class, may be somewhat surprising at first, but several points should be emphasized. First, the denominator of the ratio is small, and small changes in the numerator have a large effect. In 1950, for example, if average taxes were less by only $44 per household, the ratio would have equaled the average for all classes. (It should also be noted that, by 1970, the average burden of taxes in the lowest income class is $238 above the average burden of 33.9 percent for all classes.) Second, the numerator of the ratio includes indirect as well as direct taxes and since the share of consumption expenditures exceeds the share of factor income in the lowest class, the share of indirect taxes paid by the lowest income class is larger than their share of direct taxes. Finally, the factor income base considerably reduces the income of the poor by ignoring cash transfers received from government. For instance, average money income is $600 higher than factor income for the lowest class in 1970. If money income is substituted for factor income, tax ratios in the lowest class decrease to 23.8, 21.1, and 37.3 percent in 1950, 1961, and 1970, respectively, which approximate the averages among all households in each year.

The character of the tax burden ratios appears to have changed somewhat over time. In 1950, the lowest relative burden occurs in the income class just above the lowest, although it is not much below the average of 21.6 percent, which is also the case for the other middle-income classes. In 1961, however, the middle-income classes converge even closer, with the lowest ratio no longer occurring in the class just above the lowest. The 1970 numbers show a monotonic decline in relative tax burden up to the highest class, although the differences are trivial in classes 8 through 10 ($8000–$25,000), which contain more than two-thirds of the income. In fact, all these comparisons must be made very carefully because the proportions of households and income by class are different each year. The lowest and highest classes, however, are always of interest, and they are comparable across years.

In sharp contrast to taxes, the expenditure pattern is quite pro-poor, under standard incidence assumptions, at least relative to income in each class. Each year shows a similar monotonic decline in the ratio of direct and indirect expenditures received as income increases. This is because expenditures increase very slowly with income; government expenditures are relatively income inelastic in terms of a cross-section profile. It is difficult to draw any further inferences about the relative pattern of the temporal increase in expenditures by income class without statistical measures of the changes.

Of course, altering incidence assumptions will change the picture presented in table 4.2. One plausible change is to distribute the general expenditures of government entirely by factor income rather than by the distribution of households. Table 4.3 shows the decrease in the pro-poor nature of expenditures if this neutral form of indivisible expenditures is assumed. Although government output is distributed in a less pro-poor manner under this assumption, the pro-poor distribution of expenditures is still preserved. Intertemporal comparisons also appear not to change.

On the tax side of the budget, many plausible incidence assumptions are possible, but before considering how these might change our intertemporal comparisons, let us turn to the regression framework.[6]

The Regression Framework

Regressions pose some terminological and conceptual issues which had best receive explicit treatment at the outset. Both taxes and benefits are defined as progressive when the ratio of taxes paid or benefits received to

---

[6] The Appendixes allow interested readers to construct many more ratios of taxes and/or expenditures to income.

TABLE 4.3

Expenditures as a Percentage of Factor Income,
General Expenditures Distributed by Factor Income,
1950, 1961, and 1970

Income Class	$\left(\dfrac{\text{Expenditures}}{\text{Factor Income}}\right) \times 100$		
	1950	1961	1970
$0–$1000	125.2	} 120.0	} 211.2
1000–$2000	29.2		
2000–$3000	21.6	67.6	139.5
3000–$4000	19.4	45.2	98.0
4000–$5000	17.1	33.4	73.7
5000–$6000	} 16.6	30.6	53.2
6000–$7000		} 28.4	43.4
7000–$7500			} 38.1
7500–$8000	} 14.7	} 26.2	
8000–$10,000			34.7
10,000–$15,000		25.2	30.8
15,000–$25,000		} 23.8	26.6
25,000+			23.7
Total	20.3	31.4	35.4

SOURCES: Appendixes B, C, and E.

income rises as income rises. Thus progressive taxes favor lower income groups, while progressive benefits favor higher income groups. Because this terminology seems awkward, we tend to substitute the term "pro-rich" for regressive taxes and progressive benefits, and "pro-poor" for progressive taxes and regressive benefits.

With linear tax and expenditure functions, marginal benefit tax rates are constant, and whether a function is regressive, progressive, or neutral depends only upon the intercept of the function. For any nonzero intercept, the average tax rate will asymptotically approach the constant marginal tax rate as income increases.[7] In our comparisons, average income increased over time, which implies that the degree of progression in the tax structure, or regression in the benefit structure, would decline over time if the intercept and slopes of the functions remained stable. The higher incomes

[7] Write taxes, T, as a linear function of income, $T = a + bY$. The marginal tax rate is constant, $dT/dY = b$, and the average tax rate is $T/Y = a/Y + b$ which varies with income if the intercept is nonzero, $d/(T/Y)dY = -a/Y^2$. The average tax will rise, stay constant, or decline with income if and only if the intercept is negative, zero, or positive. For discussions of progressivity, see Musgrave and Musgrave (1973, pp. 261–63); and Johansen (1968, pp. 211–15).

become, the closer we approach proportional tax and expenditure functions, ceteris paribus.

The first set of comparisons are weighted, ordinary least squares regressions with dollars gained (or lost) as the dependent variable and mean factor income per income class as the independent variable for each year.[8] The intercepts are the estimated dollars' worth of gain or loss at zero income and the slope coefficients are the cents' worth of change in either expenditures or taxes per dollar increase in income; the slope is the effective expenditure rate or tax rate with respect to income. Although intercepts and slopes are often discussed separately, recall that if the intercept is known, the slope is also known (and vice versa) because the regression line must intersect the means of both variables.

Some use is also made of log-linear regressions in this chapter which, of course, produce constant elasticity estimates. It is conventional to characterize such tax functions as progressive when the elasticity exceeds one and regressive when it is less than one, and vice versa for expenditure functions.

Factor Income Regression

Table 4.4 shows the linear regression results for the tax and expenditure functions with respect to factor income, with the standard incidence assumptions, and no adjustment for inflation. Comparing the slope coefficients along row 9 of table 4.4 reveals that the net fiscal incidence function (the expenditures schedule minus the tax schedule) became slightly steeper between 1950 and 1961 ($-.20$ versus $-.24$), but did not steepen perceptibly between 1961 and 1970 ($-.24$ versus $-.25$). Intercepts shifted up considerably in both decades, more than doubling between 1950 and 1961 and almost doubling again between 1961 and 1970, a total increase from less than $1000 in 1950 to over $3500 in 1970. Upward shifts in the intercept are to the relative advantage of households at the low end of the distribution, although only 11 percent were below $2000 income by 1970 compared with 33 percent in 1950.

The shifts in tax and expenditure functions which produced these changes in net fiscal incidence are illustrated in figure 4.1. The most obvious feature is the dramatic upward shifts in the expenditure functions, although the expenditure functions for 1961 and 1970 also have steeper slopes than in 1950. An increase over time in both the intercept and slope for expenditure

---

[8] The observations are weighted by the frequency distribution of households to ensure that the regression lines intersect the true means obtained from individual observations (Cramer 1969, pp. 144–45). An earlier version used an unweighted comparison (Reynolds and Smolensky 1974).

TABLE 4.4

Tax and Expenditure Regressions with Factor Income, Standard Incidence (Current Dollars)

Dependent Variable	Intercept 1950	Intercept 1961	Intercept 1970	Slope 1950	Slope 1961	Slope 1970	R^2 1950	R^2 1961	R^2 1970
State and local									
1. Expenditures	201	593	1358	.02	.04	.05	.48	.98	.96
2. Taxes	57	222	353	.05	.08	.10	.99	.99	.99
3. Net	144	372	1004	−.04	−.04	−.05	.75	.99	.97
Federal									
4. Expenditures	431	1101	1881	.06	.08	.06	.97	.91	.79
5. Taxes	−361	−628	−647	.22	.28	.26	.97	.93	.94
6. Net	791	1729	2527	−.16	−.20	−.20	.95	.92	.95
Total									
7. Expenditures	632	1694	3238	.08	.12	.11	.92	.96	.90
8. Taxes	−304	−407	−293	.28	.35	.36	.98	.96	.97
9. Net	936	2101	3531	−.20	−.24	−.25	.98	.95	.96
10. Expenditures per household	1030	2694	4657	—	—	—	—	—	—
11. Proportional	—	—	—	.22	.31	.34	—	—	—

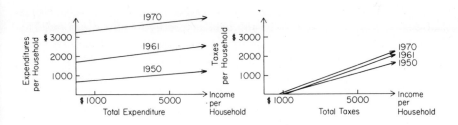

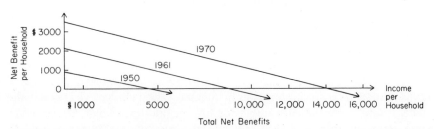

FIGURE 4.1 *Expenditure, taxes, and net benefit regressions with factor income, standard incidence, 1950, 1961, 1970 (current dollars).*

functions creates something of a problem in interpretation. At first blush, it would seem that a rise in the expenditure intercept is pro-poor and a rise in the slope is pro-rich. This kind of inference is complicated, however, by the increase in mean income over time and the decreasing number of households with income under $2000 over time. In a sense, the intercept serves only as an indicator of the level of government rather than a relative distributive index. For instance, between 1950 and 1961 government expenditures per household increased by 162 percent and the expenditure intercept grew by 168 percent. Similarly, government expenditures per household grew by 73 percent and the expenditure intercept grew by 91 percent from 1961 to 1970 (row 10 in table 4.4). Thus in both decades, the expenditure intercept appears to increase much like growth in expenditures per household. In the first decade, the total expenditure slope steepened but fell slightly in the second decade (row 7). This does not lend itself easily to distributive interpretation because both periods are dominated by the upward shift in the distribution of households. In each year, expenditures are very pro-poor in the sense that intercepts are relatively large and expenditure slopes are only one-third as large as those for an expenditure system proportional to factor income.

The tax functions lie closer together than do the expenditure functions. The largest difference among slopes is between the small coefficient in 1950 (.28) and the larger coefficients in 1961 (.35) and 1970 (.36). Row 11 in table 4.4 shows the regression line for a tax system which would be effectively proportional to income—zero intercepts and marginal tax rates of .22, .31, and .34 in 1950, 1961, and 1970, respectively. The estimated slopes of .28, .35, and .36 appear to be approaching proportionality over time. The negative tax intercept fell between 1950 and 1961 but rose between 1961 and 1970. A heroic interpretation would be that the U.S. tax structure became more pro-poor between 1950 and 1961 but less pro-poor during the 1960s, although the dollar changes are very small, as is readily apparent in figure 4.1. A more interesting interpretation is that the income level at which all taxes become effectively positive (an implicit exemption level) did not noticeably move in two decades, despite the inflation over the period.

At the state and local level, table 4.4 shows that the expenditure intercept increased more than sixfold between 1950 and 1970 and that the positive tax intercept also increased more than fivefold, which produced a sixfold increase in net fiscal incidence at zero income. Note, however, the low R^2 (.48) for the state-local expenditure regression, indicating a poor fit of expenditures as a linear function of income. The intercept changes at the federal level were both favorable for low-income households; the expenditure intercept increased threefold and the negative tax intercept was 80 percent less, which together produced a twofold increase in net fiscal incidence.

The net slope coefficient for the average state and local government changed in favor of the poor because an adverse rise in the benefit slope was slightly more than offset by a favorable rise in the tax slope. The federal coefficients show virtually no rise in the benefit slope and a steeper tax slope which together produced a steeper (more pro-poor) slope for net incidence.

In summary, the net effect of the myriad changes in tax and expenditure practice over two decades can be characterized as follows: Households faced somewhat steeper tax schedules over time, and rising incomes generated much larger revenues and expenditures by government. The benefits of these expenditures accrued to the low end of the distribution as well as the high end, but any shifts in the distributive pattern of expenditures are difficult to detect with linear regressions. For example, average government expenditures received in the lowest income class grew by 216 percent from 1950 to 1970, but during the same period, average benefits received in the highest income class grew by 286 percent. Meanwhile, average taxes paid in the lowest income class increased by 226 percent while they increased by 248 percent in the highest income class. The net effect was rather similar between the lowest and highest income classes because net benefits increased by 214 percent in the lowest income class while net taxes increased by 223 percent in the highest class, consistent with the largely parallel shifts in the net incidence function in table 4.4 (row 9).

One potentially misleading aspect of the regression analysis thus far is that the data are not adjusted for changes in the price level. Of course any rescaling of the data to real terms, assuming the same price index for each income class, changes only the intercept estimate, not the slope or R^2. To adjust for inflation, the intercepts have been stated in terms of constant 1967 dollars in table 4.5.[9] Obviously, the differences among intercepts are smaller than previously. Graphically, the tax and expenditure functions are closer together, relative to those in figure 4.1, but no qualitative conclusions are modified. Subsequent intercepts are not adjusted for inflation.

[9] Column 3 in the table below shows the adjustment factor that produced table 4.5 from table 4.4:

	(1) Consumer Price Index	(2) Wholesale Price Index	(3) $100.00/ Consumer Price Index
	(1967 = 100)	(1967 = 100)	(1967 = $1.00)
1950	72.1	81.8	$1.387
1961	89.6	94.5	1.116
1970	116.3	110.4	.860

SOURCE: U.S. Council of Economic Advisers (1972, pp. 247, 250).

TABLE 4.5

Tax and Expenditure Regressions with Factor Income, Standard Incidence
(Constant 1967 Dollars)

Dependent Variable (per Household)	Intercept			Slope		
	1950	1961	1970	1950	1961	1970
State and local						
1. Expenditures	279	662	1168	.02	.04	.05
2. Taxes	79	248	304	.05	.08	.10
3. Net	200	415	863	−.04	−.04	−.05
Federal						
4. Expenditures	598	1229	1618	.06	.08	.06
5. Taxes	−501	−701	−556	.22	.28	.26
6. Net	1097	1930	2173	−.16	−.20	−.20
Total						
7. Expenditures	877	1891	2785	.08	.12	.11
8. Taxes	−422	−454	−252	.28	.35	.36
9. Net	1298	2345	3037	−.20	−.24	−.25

General Expenditures by Income

Now consider some departures from the standard incidence assumptions. Table 4.6 results from an experiment in which all the standard assumptions are preserved except that the general expenditures of government are entirely distributed by initial factor income (w/o GE). This would reflect a belief that the indivisible expenditures of government are neutral with respect to the distribution of income rather than redistributing in favor of lower incomes. National defense is the largest component of general expenditures and Earl Thompson (1974) provides indirect support for distributing general expenditures by factor income or a similar series by arguing that the private accumulation of certain kinds of capital creates an extra defense burden because it is coveted by potential foreign aggressors. He further argues that the entire U.S. tax structure approximates an a priori, Pareto-optimal one which appropriately assesses user charges upon creators of private capital.

The tax functions of table 4.6 are unchanged from table 4.4, but the expenditure functions have reduced intercepts and steeper slopes. This obviously produces net fiscal incidence functions with smaller intercepts and less negative slopes, that is, net government output is distributed in a less pro-poor manner under these new incidence assumptions.

For comparative purposes, the expenditure functions for 1950 and 1970 are depicted in figure 4.2. It shows the modest decrease in the pro-poor dis-

TABLE 4.6

*Tax and Expenditure Regressions with Factor Income, Standard Incidence
Except General Expenditures by Income (Current Dollars)*

Dependent Variable (per Household)	Intercept			Slope		
	1950	1961	1970	1950	1961	1970
State and local						
1. Expenditures	170	433	1027	.02[a]	.06	.07
2. Taxes	57	222	353	.05	.08	.10
3. Net	113	212	674	−.03[b]	−.02	−.03
Federal						
4. Expenditures	221	552	1129	.10	.14	.12
5. Taxes	−361	−628	−647	.22	.28	.26
6. Net	582	1180	1776	−.12	−.13	−.15
Total						
7. Expenditures	391	985	2156	.13	.20	.19
8. Taxes	−304	−407	−293	.28	.35	.36
9. Net	695	1392	2450	−.15	−.15	−.17

NOTE: All R^2's exceed .84 except where specifically noted.
[a] $R^2 = .63$.
[b] $R^2 = .67$.

tribution of government benefits when general expenditures are allocated in proportion to income.

Regressive Incidence

The next experiment substitutes a set of regressive tax incidence assumptions into the previous experiment. All expenditures are distributed in the standard way except that general government expenditures are distributed by factor income. The incidence assumptions for two taxes are changed from the standard.[10] First, corporate income taxes are entirely shifted forward to consumption expenditures. In addition, 60 percent of property taxes are distributed by housing expenditures, and 40 percent by consumption expenditures, a slightly more regressive distribution. Table 4.7 reports the new regression estimates. The expenditure coefficients are the same as in table 4.6 but tax intercepts are increased and the slopes decline, predictably enough. A more interesting observation is that there are no sizable changes at the state and local level, but there are very noticeable changes at the

[10] Several other inconsequential changes were also made. For 1970, estate and gift taxes were distributed by estate and gift income. For 1950 and 1961 sales and excise taxes were also distributed by consumption.

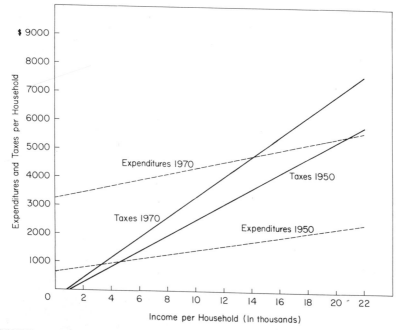

FIGURE 4.2 *Expenditure and tax regressions with factor income, standard incidence, 1950, 1970 (current dollars).*

federal level. Tax intercepts increase by about $400 and marginal tax rates decline by 18 percent, for example, from .26 to .22 for federal taxes in 1970. Both changes are adverse to low-income recipients. The large effect of regressive incidence assumptions upon the federal tax functions produces a significant shift against the poor in the regression line for net fiscal incidence. Net fiscal incidence appears therefore to be sensitive to the choice of incidence assumptions in each year. It should be noted however that the change due to altering the tax incidence assumptions are quite similar for each year. Intertemporal comparisons are virtually unaffected.

Progressive Incidence

The next experiment adopts relatively progressive incidence assumptions. The changes from the normal assumptions are: the corporate income tax and sales-excise taxes are distributed 33 percent by dividends, 33 percent by wages and salaries, and 34 percent by consumption expenditures; the Social Security tax is distributed 50 percent by the employee payroll tax, 25 percent by dividends, and 25 percent by consumption expenditures; and

TABLE 4.7

Tax and Expenditure Regressions with Factor Income, Regressive Incidence
(Current Dollars)

Dependent Variable (per Household)	Intercept			Slope		
	1950	1961	1970	1950	1961	1970
State and Local						
1. Expenditures	170	433	1027	.02[a]	.06	.07
2. Taxes	71	237	453	.05	.08	.09
3. Net	99	196	574	−.03[b]	−.02	−.02
Federal						
4. Expenditures	221	552	1129	.10	.14	.12
5. Taxes	−138	−271	−104	.18	.23	.22
6. Net	360	823	1233	−.08	−.09	−.10
Total						
7. Expenditures	391	985	2156	.13	.20	.19
8. Taxes	−68	−34	349	.23	.31	.31
9. Net	459	1019	1808	−.10	−.11	−.12

NOTE: All R^2's exceed .82 except where specifically noted.
[a] $R^2 = .63$.
[b] $R^2 = .62$.

property taxes are distributed 40 percent by housing expenditures, 30 percent by dividends, and 30 percent by consumption expenditures.[11] All expenditures are distributed in the standard way except for general expenditures which are assigned according to the distribution of households. These incidence assumptions shift the regression lines by large amounts, as the numbers in table 4.8 reveal. For example, relative to the standard incidence of table 4.4, expenditure intercepts rise by one-third and expenditure slopes decrease by over 50 percent. Tax functions also shift dramatically; for instance, tax slopes rise by about 25 percent. The intertemporal comparisons remain unaltered, however: expenditure functions shift upward over time and tax functions steepen.

Whatever the incidence assumptions, the regression analyses of this chapter lead to the same qualitative conclusion: the period was marked by households moving along a steepening tax schedule accompanied by much higher government expenditures from which the low end of the distribution benefited as well as the middle and high ends. In the next chapter, the effect of this process on final income inequality will be explicitly examined.

[11] The progressive distribution of property taxes reflects recent arguments that some part of these taxes are borne by all owners of capital in the economy; see Aaron et al. (1974).

TABLE 4.8
Tax and Expenditure Regressions with Factor Income, Progressive Incidence (Current Dollars)

Dependent Variable (per Household)	Intercept			Slope			R^2		
	1950	1961	1970	1950	1961	1970	1950	1961	1970
State and local									
1. Expenditures	232	753	1688	.01	.02	.02	.26	.94	.84
2. Taxes	−145	−256	−505	.09	.13	.16	.95	.90	.90
3. Net	378	1010	2193	−.08	−.11	−.14	.95	.85	.86
Federal									
4. Expenditures	640	1650	2632	.02	.01	.00	.80	.24	.01
5. Taxes	−484	−831	−1072	.25	.30	.30	.96	.90	.91
6. Net	1124	2482	3703	−.23	−.29	−.29	.96	.93	.94
Total									
7. Expenditures	873	2404	4320	.03	.03	.03	.63	.69	.33
8. Taxes	−629	−1088	−1576	.34	.43	.46	.95	.90	.91
9. Net	1502	3491	5896	−.31	−.40	−.43	.97	.91	.92

Money Income Regressions and Elasticity Estimates

To complete the regression comparisons, we examine the consequences of substituting money income for factor income as the independent variable in the linear regressions. We also look at some elasticity estimates. Table 4.9 shows the results for money income using standard incidence assumptions. The regressions are conceptually identical to those in table 4.4 except for the income base. The expenditure regressions in tables 4.9 and 4.4 are nearly identical because expenditure intercepts and slopes are unaffected by the shift in income bases. The tax functions of table 4.9, however, are all steeper than for factor income (table 4.4), and have lower intercepts. In other words, the money income base makes the total tax system appear more pro-poor in each year than did the factor income regressions.

The explanation for this result is that substituting money income as the base reduces average income in the top income brackets and raises it in low income brackets (Appendix C). The amount of taxes in each bracket, however, is unchanged because taxes are allocated on the basis of an unchanged set of distributors. These two features necessarily imply a steepening of the regression line summarizing the tax–income relationship. The net result is also a steepening of the net fiscal incidence slope, shown in the bottom row of table 4.9. Additional linear regressions with money income (not shown here) produced the same results—negligible changes in expenditure functions and sizable steepening of tax functions.

TABLE 4.9
Tax and Expenditure Regressions with Money Income, Standard Incidence (Current Dollars)

Dependent Variable (per Household)	Intercept			Slope			R^2		
	1950	1961	1970	1950	1961	1970	1950	1961	1970
State and local									
1. Expenditures	198	590	1295	.02	.04	.05	.36	.97	.95
2. Taxes	−8	205	93	.07	.08	.12	.97	.97	.97
3. Net	206	386	1202	−.05	−.04	−.07	.81	.95	.91
Federal									
4. Expenditures	413	1079	1928	.07	.08	.06	.95	.92	.68
5. Taxes	−593	−768	−1191	.27	.29	.31	.89	.97	.84
6. Net	1005	1847	3119	−.20	−.21	−.25	.86	.97	.84
Total									
7. Expenditures	611	1669	3223	.08	.12	.11	.85	.97	.84
8. Taxes	−601	−563	−1098	.33	.37	.42	.91	.99	.88
9. Net	1212	2232	4321	−.25	−.25	−.31	.91	.98	.86

Elasticity estimates are presented in table 4.10. Except for state and local expenditures in 1950, income elasticities are always significant at the one percent level but one-half of the R^2's are below .80, especially for expenditure and net incidence elasticities. In other words, these should be

TABLE 4.10
Elasticities for Standard Post-Fisc, Factor and Money Income

Dependent Variable	1950		1961		1970	
	Factor	Money	Factor	Money	Factor	Money
State and local						
1. Expenditures	.02[a]	.00[a]	.29	.36	.23	.26
2. Taxes	.78	.85	.70	.90	.64	.74
3. Net	.00	−.01	−.03[a]	−.04	−.01[a]	−.01[a]
Federal						
4. Expenditures	.27[a]	.27[a]	.21[a]	.26[a]	.15[a]	.16[a]
5. Taxes	1.02	1.10	1.08	1.39	.98	1.15
6. Net	−.01[a]	−.01[a]	−.14[a]	−.21[a]	−.04[a]	−.04[a]
Total						
7. Expenditures	.19[a]	.18[a]	.24[a]	.29	.18[a]	.20[a]
8. Taxes	.94	1.02	.92	1.19	.82	.95
9. Net	−.02[a]	−.02[a]	−.18[a]	−.27[a]	−.05[a]	−.06[a]

[a] R^2 below .80.

interpreted cautiously because elasticities may not summarize the relationships very well. The tax functions, however, fit very well, with R^2's always exceeding .94. There are two interesting features about table 4.10. First, expenditure elasticities are always far below unit elasticity; in other words, expenditures are "redistributive" in the sense that they are less than proportional to income. Also, expenditure elasticities exhibit no trend over time, which can be interpreted as saying that total expenditures are not increasingly redistributive toward households with low market incomes over time. Note also that the expenditure elasticity has not fallen to zero, perhaps an egalitarian benchmark. If general expenditures are distributed according to income, total expenditure elasticities nearly double but are below .4 in 1970. Also, money income expenditure elasticities appear somewhat higher than factor income, but the differences are trivial.

Tax elasticities also do not seem to be changing much over time. According to table 4.10, tax elasticities were not very different within these three years, although there is a slight trend away from progressivity of the overall tax system between 1950 and 1970. Within each year, tax elasticities are higher with respect to money income than factor income.

Although R^2's are relatively low for net fiscal incidence functions, generally about .40, the elasticities do not show any trend in the net redistributive power of government. In 1950, for instance, the net incidence elasticity was about −.02 and by 1970 it was −.05. This interpretation may be unwarranted because of the poor fit, but we return to this issue.

5

Further Results: Gini Concentration Ratios and Lorenz Curves

Differences among Lorenz curves based on different, but apparently equally good, methods and sources are of the same order of magnitude as differences among Lorenz curves for different years. [M. Friedman; Brady 1951, p. 57]

The Gini concentration ratio will be used in this chapter to compare the dispersion in initial and final distributions within and across years. Of course, if distributions vary greatly in their shape, a single measure of dispersion can be misleading. For example, two Lorenz curves which intersect can be associated with identical Gini coefficients. Since some of the Lorenz curves do cross, careful interpretation is warranted, especially when differences between Gini coefficients are small.[1] The Lorenz curves are presented along with the Gini coefficients in some comparisons, reducing some of the risk. Normative interpretations of the Gini indexes are best discouraged in view of the recent work relating various inequality orderings to social welfare functions.[2] There is, however, no summary statistic which is superior on every plausible criterion. Its strengths and weaknesses are well known primarily because it is the most popular and, hence, the most familiar relevant summary statistic. Familiarity was indeed the decisive factor leading to our use of it.

The strength of a summary statistic is also its weakness. Changes in Gini coefficients can be due to changes in the shape of the distribution at the low end, in the middle, or at the high end. Simulations by Champernowne (1974) suggest that the Gini ratio is relatively sensitive to inequality within the middle-income ranges. Progress in discovering the properties of measures of dispersion continues, but more important for present purposes

---

[1] For evidence that the Gini ratio is sensitive to distributive changes, see Gastwirth (1972) and Champernowne (1974). For a contrary assertion, see Watts and Peck (1975).

[2] See Atkinson (1970), Sheshinski (1972), and Dasgupta, Sen, and Starret (1973).

is the problem of accurately estimating Gini ratios for grouped data. Since the observed range of variation within a country is small compared to sampling errors, the estimation technique deserves attention as an additional source of error. The computed approximations of the concentration ratio have a bias that makes the numerical estimates systematically too low. The Gini estimates are lower bounds on the true concentration ratio because income variability within groups is neglected.[3] This bias is smaller the more observations there are, although it is not necessarily optimal that they be evenly spaced for distributions typically skewed to the right (Gastwirth 1972). Unfortunately, the number of groups required to achieve a close bound is typically quite large (20+). The underestimate in IRS data with 25 or 26 intervals is .002 or .003, but if the intervals are reduced to 18 or 19 the underestimate is .005 or .006 (Gastwirth 1972).

Our data of course have far fewer intervals than are necessary for such small magnitudes of error. The Gini coefficients for 1950 are likely to be the most seriously underestimated, because the data are limited to only seven intervals. However, this chapter is not restricted to comparisons of aggregate Gini ratios estimated via trapezoidal approximations. We also fit a functional form to the data for each year, permitting percentile comparisons and statistical tests for differences in distributions between years, as well as providing an additional check on the estimated concentration ratios. Our conclusion that post-fisc distributions from 1950 to 1970 are quite similar is robust enough to survive both estimation techniques.

Post-Fisc Distributions with Factor'Income

Table 5.1 shows Gini ratios for the five distributive experiments discussed in chapter 4. The assumptions for the first variant, the standard incidence case, were summarized in table 4.1. The Gini coefficients produced by this normal post-fisc experiment are much smaller than the pre-fisc coefficients in each year. By this measure there are sizable redistributions of net output toward the lower end of the income distribution in each year due to government activity. Post-fisc dispersion is smallest for 1970 (339), followed by 1961 (342), and 1950 (363). Note, however, that the post-fisc Gini for 1950 is only 7 percent larger than the lowest Gini ratio, 1970. The difference between initial and post-fisc Gini coefficients was smallest in 1950 and largest in 1970, which might be interpreted as evidence that the redistributive impact of government was smallest in 1950 and largest in 1970, but more on this later.

---

[3] Bronfenbrenner (1971, pp. 49–51) illustrates the trapezoidal approximations used to estimate primary Gini coefficients in chapter 5.

TABLE 5.1
Gini Coefficients for Selected Experiments, 1950, 1961, and 1970,
Factor NNP

Distributive Experiment	Gini × 1000		
	1950	1961	1970
1. Initial factor NNP	436	436	446
2. Standard	363	342	339
3. Standard except general expenditures by income	384	378	375
4. Regressive	394	388	384
5. Progressive	328	289	284
Column mean	381	367	366

Row 3 results from the experiment in which normal incidence assumptions are preserved except that the general expenditures of government are distributed according to factor income alone (w/o GE). That is, in this experiment the indivisible expenditures of government are neutral rather than pro-poor. The effect is to substantially reduce the difference in post-fisc concentration ratios between 1950 and 1961 but the trivial difference between the post-fisc Gini ratios of 1961 and 1970 is unchanged. In other words, the relatively small post-fisc Gini coefficients for 1961 and 1970 are not preserved once general expenditures are no longer presumed to be redistributive. General expenditures at the federal level tripled between 1950 and 1961 and at the state–local level they grew even more rapidly, exceeding a fourfold increase.

The next experiment distributes expenditures in the normal way except that general government expenditures are distributed by factor income, and the incidence assumptions for two taxes are changed from the standard and made more regressive. In particular, corporate income taxes are shifted forward entirely to consumption expenditures; and 60 percent of property taxes are distributed by housing expenditures, and 40 percent by consumption expenditures. These more regressive tax assumptions raise Gini coefficients by only ten points in each year (row 4), compared to the normal with neutral general expenditures (row 3). These are very small increases in income inequality, as measured by Gini coefficients. The equal rise in the Gini in each year leaves the trend in the post-fisc distribution unaffected.

The next experiment adopts relatively progressive incidence assumptions. The changes from the standard assumptions are: the corporate income and sales-excise taxes are distributed 33 percent by dividends, 33 percent by wages and salaries, and 34 percent by consumption expenditures; the Social Security tax is distributed 50 percent by the employee payroll tax, 25 percent by dividends, 25 percent by consumption expenditures; and property taxes are distributed 40 percent by housing expenditures, 30 percent by dividends, and 30 percent by consumption expenditures. All expenditures are distributed in the standard pattern except for general expenditures, which are assigned according to the distribution of households, a strong equalizing assumption. These incidence assumptions lower the concentration ratios a considerable amount compared with standard assumptions (row 2 minus row 5): 35 points for 1950, 53 points for 1961, and 55 points for 1970. Distributing the large increase in general expenditures between 1950 and 1961 according to the distributions of households is the major factor producing this trend.

The Lorenz diagrams in figures 5.1 to 5.3 depict the cumulative share of income for the factor income base and standard post-fisc for each year. Similarity in shape across years is obvious. Figure 5.4 plots post-fisc Lorenz curves (standard incidence) for all three years. Again shapes are similar, and consequently the comparisons of Gini coefficients are not misleading.

To summarize these experiments based upon factor NNP, as well as others not reported here, post-fisc distributions are more equal in all years than are the distributions of factor income. Post-fisc inequality is lowest in

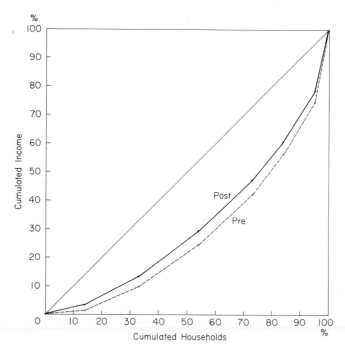

FIGURE 5.1 *Lorenz curve comparisons, factor income, standard incidence, pre- and post-fisc, 1950.*

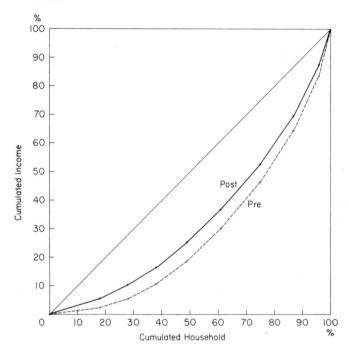

FIGURE 5.2 *Lorenz curve comparisons, factor income, standard incidence, pre- and post-fisc, 1961.*

1970 but the difference between years is trivial in most comparisons, particularly when compared to the differences between the pre-fisc and post-fisc distributions in any year.[4] Finally, the variation in Gini coefficients as incidence assumptions are altered is smallest in 1950 and largest in 1970. This is confirmed by the range of coefficients reported in table 5.1, as well as by the variance of coefficients among a larger set of experiments. Obviously this is related to the increased share of government in NNP in more recent years.

Post-Fisc Distributions with Money Income

Table 5.2 shows results for the same distributive experiments presented in table 5.1 except that the initial income distribution is based upon money

[4] Statistical tests for significant differences are presented below. We should note that one calculation which incorporated somewhat different incidence assumptions produced similar results. Corporate income taxes and property taxes were distributed according to the distribution of capital ownership in general, defined as factor income minus wages and salaries. Changes in intertemporal comparisons were trivial. For example, the Gini ratio for the standard case rose from 363 to 366 in 1950 and fell from 339 to 335 in 1970.

income (Appendix C). The initial Gini coefficients are about 10 percent smaller than those for factor earnings and 1970 once again has the highest initial Gini coefficient, but by a trivial margin over 1961.

If normal incidence assumptions are adopted, post-fisc Gini coefficients are substantially lower than they are for initial money income, just as was true for factor earnings (row 2). The decreases are nearly identical to those for factor earnings in table 5.1. If general expenditures are assigned according to money income (row 3), Gini coefficients rise above the normal post-fisc distributions by slightly smaller amounts than in table 5.1.

Row 4 reports the results for the regressive distribution of taxes. Post-fisc Gini coefficients increase by about 10 points compared to row 3, just as they did with factor earnings in table 5.1. If progressive tax assumptions are used, the Gini coefficients drop below the normal post-fisc distribution in about the same fashion as in table 5.1 (row 5). In sum, the only difference in distributive results with a money income base is a decrease of 40 points or about 10 percent in the size of the initial Gini coefficients and hence a decrease of about 50 points in all the corresponding post-fisc measures. Choosing between these income bases might be important if we wanted to

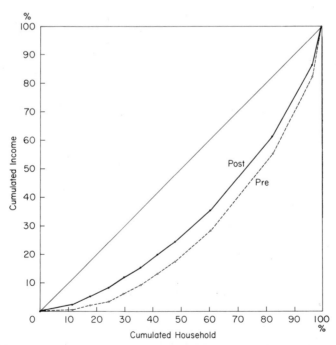

FIGURE 5.3 *Lorenz curve comparisons, factor income, standard incidence, pre- and post-fisc, 1970.*

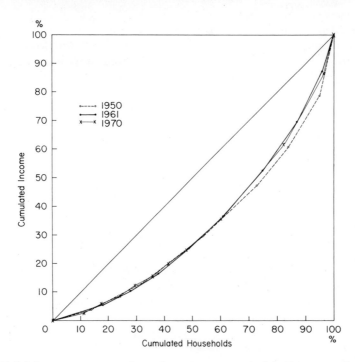

FIGURE 5.4 *Lorenz curve comparisons, factor income, standard incidence, post-fisc, 1950, 1961, 1970.*

TABLE 5.2

Gini Coefficients for Selected Experiments, 1950, 1961, 1970, Money NNP

Distributive Experiment	Gini × 1000		
	1950	1961	1970
1. Initial money NNP	391	398	400
2. Standard	315	300	290
3. Standard except general expenditures by income	334	333	322
4. Regressive	344	343	331
5. Progressive	282	251	239
Column mean	333	325	316

know what the "true" magnitude of post-fisc income dispersion is, but the choice is relatively unimportant if we are concerned only with intertemporal comparisons. Both bases tell the same intertemporal story in the aggregate. A less aggregate analysis is presented in the next chapter.

Predicted Shares

To extend the analysis, we have fitted the data to a particular functional form. The purpose is, first, to facilitate estimation of the share of income received by various proportions of households, and second, to statistically test for the significance of differences among distributions. The functional form fitted was suggested by Kakwani and Podder (1973):

$$\eta = \pi e^{-\beta(1-\pi)}, \tag{5-1}$$

where η is cumulative proportion of income, and π is cumulative proportion of households. If $\beta = 0$, the Lorenz curve coincides with the income equality line, and if $\beta > 0$, the curve lies below the income equality line.

The Gini coefficient (G) for this function is

$$G = 1 - \frac{2(\beta - 1)}{\beta^2} - \frac{2e^{-\beta}}{\beta^2} \tag{5-2}$$

for $\beta > 0$. If $\beta = 0$, the Gini ratio equals zero. If $\beta = \infty$, the Gini ratio equals one.

Table 5.3 presents selected results for fitting the data to this Lorenz function (equation [5-1]) by ordinary least squares (OLS). The initial factor income and normal post-fisc results are shown for each year.

The column named "trapezoidal Gini" shows the coefficients used thus far, which have been calculated by the method of trapezoidal approximations. This technique produces lower bound estimates for Gini coefficients, and the error generally decreases as the number of income classes increases. The last column, "OLS Gini," shows the coefficients calculated from equation (5-2). The estimated OLS Gini coefficients are generally larger than the "trapezoidal Ginis" but the differences are quite small for post-fisc distributions. Note, however, that the OLS Ginis are not required to exceed the trapezoidal Ginis because the OLS coefficients can either overestimate or underestimate.

The estimated β parameters permit the pre- and post-fisc distributions to be shown rather easily in terms of quintiles or deciles. Because the income intervals and corresponding shares of households are different for each year some kind of interpolation is required. Table 5.4 shows the predicted shares for quintiles that can be calculated from the β parameters of table 5.3. These results coincide with the rankings discussed earlier. The most striking

TABLE 5.3
Lorenz Estimation Results, 1950, 1961, and 1970

Distributive Experiment	$\hat{\beta}$	t-ratio	R^2	Trapezoidal Gini	OLS Gini
1950, n = 7					
Initial factor	2.15	14.04	.97	436	452
Standard post-fisc	1.43	21.33	.99	363	345
Normal w/o GE	1.59	20.77	.99	384	372
1961, n = 9					
Initial factor	2.25	23.36	.99	436	465
Standard post-fisc	1.42	47.27	.99	342	344
Normal w/o GE	1.69	35.06	.99	378	388
1970, n = 11					
Initial factor	2.41	21.24	.98	446	484
Standard post-fisc	1.36	40.81	.99	339	333
Normal w/o GE	1.64	31.05	.99	375	380

feature of table 5.4 is the virtual constancy of post-fisc shares by quintile. The factor income shares reveal modest declines for the lowest quintile as well as the middle 60 percent and a corresponding rise in the top quintile, as well as the top 5 percent. Post-fisc distributions reveal no trend, which is the same result we have encountered time and time again.

Significance Tests

Comparisons among Gini coefficients have thus far been confined to informal statements such as one coefficient is "substantially lower" than another or is "virtually equivalent" to another. Now we can consider a formal statistical test for differences in income dispersion between alternative years or for differences among distributions in the same year. The underlying economic rationale for such a test is that if economic relations were unchanged, income distributions should be identical except for chance variation. In other words, Gini coefficients should not differ significantly if structural relationships have not been altered.

One way to formalize this concept is to use equation (5-1) and, in general, hypothesize that

$$\hat{\beta}_{1950} = \hat{\beta}_{1961} = \hat{\beta}_{1970} = \bar{\beta}, \qquad (5-3)$$

where β is an estimate of income dispersion, and testing for equality of coefficients constitutes a test for equality of income dispersion between years or experiments. The procedure for executing this test is specified by

TABLE 5.4
Predicted Share of Income, Quintiles, 1950, 1961, and 1970

	Factor Income			Standard Post-Fisc			Standard Post-Fisc w/o GE		
Percentile Share	1950	1961	1970	1950	1961	1970	1950	1961	1970
Share of lowest 20%	3.6	3.3	2.9	6.4	6.4	6.7	5.6	5.2	5.4
Share of middle 60%	48.5	47.7	46.5	53.7	53.8	54.2	52.6	51.9	52.2
Share of highest 20%	48.0	49.0	50.6	39.9	39.8	39.1	41.8	42.9	42.4
Share of highest 5%	14.7	15.1	15.8	11.6	11.5	11.2	12.3	12.7	12.5

NOTE: All figures are percentages.

Chow (1960). The Chow test for equality of regression coefficients is an F test in which, if $F > F_\epsilon$, we reject the hypothesis that $\hat{\beta}_1 = \hat{\beta}_2 = \bar{\beta}$.

Four main results emerge from the Chow tests (see table 5.5). First, in each year, the regression coefficients for the pre-fisc distributions are statistically significantly different from the regression coefficients for the post-fisc distributions at the 5 percent level. Since the post-fisc Gini, which is a function of the regression coefficient, is smaller than the pre-fisc Gini in

TABLE 5.5
Chow Tests for Significant Differences in β Coefficients

Distributive Experiment	Factor Income F-ratio	Money Income F-ratio
1950–1950 pre- standard post-fisc	18.51*	20.09*
1961–1961 pre- standard post-fisc	67.93*	139.37*
1970–1970 pre- standard post-fisc	78.54*	91.64*
1950–1970 standard post-fisc	1.03	4.30
1950–1961 standard post-fisc	.05	13.88*
1961–1970 standard post-fisc	1.30	2.66
1950–1970 post-fisc w/o GE	.30	.20
1950–1961 post-fisc w/o GE	1.42	5.44*
1961–1970 post-fisc w/o GE	.43	3.03
1950–1970 regressive	.17	.36
1950–1961 regressive	1.79	4.28
1961–1970 regressive	1.12	1.92
1950–1970 progressive	9.82*	16.55*
1950–1961 progressive	5.21*	38.80*
1961–1970 progressive	1.88	2.69

* Significant at the 5 percent level.

each year, it may be said that post-fisc inequality (standard) is signficantly less than pre-fisc inequality, in each year. This might be interpreted as saying that the revenue and expenditure system significantly reduces final income inequality. Second, for the post-fisc inequality coefficients in each pairwise comparison, whether the standard incidence assumptions or the standard without general expenditure incidence assumptions is employed, the regression coefficients never differ significantly if we confine our attention to the factor income base. In other words, according to this statistical test, we cannot reject the hypothesis that the small observed differences in post-fisc inequality are simply due to chance variation. Two exceptions to this general characterization occur with the money income base. Inequality in 1961 is significantly lower than in 1950 in both the standard post-fisc distribution and the post-fisc with neutral general expenditures. Third, the distributions for each year are not significantly different under regressive incidence assumptions with either income base. Finally, the 1950 distribution is significantly more unequal than 1961 and 1970 under the progressive assumptions, but 1961 does not differ significantly from 1970. The explanation is that the major expansion of "general expenditures" occurred between 1950 and 1961 and, since the progressive assumptions distribute general expenditures equally to households, it lowers inequality by relatively large amounts in 1961 and 1970 but not nearly so much for 1950. Overall, the statistical tests confirm the less formal comparisons which continue to say that differences are negligible in post-fisc inequality for our three years.

6

Searching for Explanations

The stability of inequality is a source of distress to all sensitive egalitarians.
[K. Boulding 1975, p. 1]

Our empirical analysis has shown that inclusion of all government spending and taxation in household incomes significantly reduces effective income differences among income classes in each year but that dispersion in these post-fisc income distributions has not changed significantly between 1950 and 1970. That the difference between pre-fisc and post-fisc distributions is quite large each year but that the differences among post-fisc distributions are quite small raises an interesting puzzle. It appears that government spending and taxing has an equalizing effect upon households at any point in time but that a substantial rise in the government share over this twenty year period did not have the same effect. The relationship observed in the cross section does not seem to hold in the time series. Why? Why has the redistributive "bang per buck" apparently diminished in the postwar period? Although net government output is distributed in a pro-poor fashion each year, the growth of government since 1950 failed to produce a more compact distribution. This chapter explores this issue.

Stable Distributions but Rising Government

The difference between pre- and post-fisc inequality in any year was probably quite small at some time in U.S. history. Government controlled far smaller shares of national income, and it is doubtful that the tax and expenditure structure was substantially more pro-poor than today. The smaller share of government is described in table 6.1, which shows total taxes as a percentage of NNP for selected years from 1902 to 1970. Prior to 1914, taxes for all levels of government were less than 10 percent of NNP. World War I temporarily pushed the ratio above 20 percent (not shown in

TABLE 6.1

Ratio of Total Taxes to NNP, Selected
Years, 1902–1970

Year	Percentage
1902	7.2
1922	10.9
1927	10.7
1932	15.7
1936	14.1
1944	24.6
1948	21.0
1950	21.6
1961	30.5
1970	33.9

NOTE: Data for 1950, 1961, and 1970 are
from Appendixes C and D. Data for the
earlier years, which are not exactly comparable, are from U.S. Department of
Commerce (1960, pp. 139, 722).

the table), but it fell back to about 10 to 12 percent during the 1920s. The
ratio increased to about 15 percent in the 1930s partly due to a 46 percent
decrease in nominal GNP between 1929 and 1933. The ratio rose sharply
during WWII, peaking at 25 percent, then fell to about 20 percent until the
Korean War, when the ratio of taxes to NNP began a long ascent from
around 20 toward 35 percent. The ratio of expenditures to NNP would
show more violent fluctuations, especially during war periods when federal
deficits were massive, but the overall trend is, of course, similar to the trend
in tax receipts. The potential for a substantial difference between pre- and
post-fisc income distributions grew as the ratio of government taxing and
spending to NNP grew.

The difference between pre- and post-fisc inequality is now quite large.
During some period prior to 1950 the ratio of government to NNP grew
enough, and/or effective tax rates became progressive enough over a large
enough range of income, and/or benefits became pro-poor enough to make
post-fisc and pre-fisc inequality significantly different. Thus, replicating this
study with an appropriate choice of beginning and ending years would
produce quite different results from those reported in this monograph. Pre-
and post-fisc dispersion would be similar in the early year and different in
the later year. After that carefully selected but unknown terminal year, the
difference between pre- and post-fisc inequality appears to have stabilized,
despite the continual rise in the ratio of government expenditures to NNP.

The explanation must lie in a decreasingly favorable composition of expenditures or taxes for low income households over time, or else in decreasing progressivity in individual taxes and expenditures.

The Relative Size of Government

To explore these possibilities, add a time subscript, t, to equation (3-1) to produce equation (6-1):

$$c_t = \mathbf{m}_t + \mathbf{g}_t \mathbf{B}_t - \mathbf{x}_t \mathbf{T}_t \qquad (6\text{-}1)$$

where t is 0 (1950), 1 (1961), 2 (1970). All terms in equation (6-1) changed between 1950 and 1970, but we want to isolate the effect of the changing ratios of government expenditures (and taxes) to NNP. To control for the relative size of government, consider a change in the actual distribution in 1950, $c_0 = \mathbf{m}_0 + \mathbf{g}_0 \mathbf{B}_0 - \mathbf{x}_0 \mathbf{T}_0$, derived by substituting new vectors of taxes and expenditures:

$$c_{0.2} = \mathbf{m}_0 + \mathbf{g}_{0.2} \mathbf{B}_0 - \mathbf{x}_{0.2} \mathbf{T}_0, \qquad (6\text{-}2)$$

where

$c_{0.2}$ = hypothetical vector of post-fisc income if expenditures and taxes were like those of 1970,

$\mathbf{m}_0$ = vector of factor income in 1950,

$\mathbf{g}_{0.2}$ = hypothetical vector of government expenditures in 1950 if expenditures were like those of 1970,

$\mathbf{B}_0$ = matrix of 1950 distributors for expenditures,

$\mathbf{x}_{0.2}$ = hypothetical vector of government taxes in 1950 if taxes were like those of 1970,

$\mathbf{T}_0$ = matrix of 1950 distributors for taxes.

Equation (6-2) is the hypothetical distribution which would have existed in 1950 if the relative composition of government expenditures and taxes were as they were in 1970, ceteris paribus. In other words, the initial distribution of income, $\mathbf{m}_0$, distributors for benefits, $\mathbf{B}_0$, and distributors for taxes, $\mathbf{T}_0$, remain unchanged for 1950 and new dollar amounts of expenditures and taxes are substituted. The new vectors are constructed by calculating the 1970 ratio to NNP of each subcategory of expenditures and taxes and multiplying these percentages by the actual NNP of 1950 ($264 billion). The result is an increase in the 1950 ratio of government expenditures to NNP from 20 percent to 35 percent, and a shift in the relative composition of taxes and expenditures to those of 1970. There are six such permutations possible for the three years. The Gini coefficients for the standard case associated with each of these "counterbudget" experiments are reported in table 6.2, along with the three actual Gini coefficients, which appear along the diagonal.

Comparisons across rows provide a method for isolating the effect of government size upon post-fisc Gini ratios. Across any row, from left to right, the ratio of government expenditures to NNP increases, while the pre-fisc distributions and distributors are held constant for each year. This should produce lower Gini coefficients, ceteris paribus, and the expected declines are observed in each row. The sharpest increase in the relative size of government occurred in the period 1950–1961 and we might expect the largest declines in Gini coefficients to occur in the first decade. This is confirmed.

Comparisons down columns show the combined effects of changes in the distribution of expenditures and taxes, holding the size of government constant. The government share and composition of taxes and expenditures are held constant at the actual government share of NNP down columns for each year, but the pre-fisc distributions and distributors change. For example, the first column shows what the concentration ratio would have been if the level and composition of both taxes and expenditures were the same as in 1950. The Gini ratios for 1961 and 1970 are different only because the relative distribution of taxes and expenditures was either more or less equalizing than in 1950. Table 6.2 shows that Gini coefficients rise monotonically by year for each standardized budget. This means that the distributive matrices for government taxes and/or expenditures are most equalizing in 1950 and least effective in terms of reducing inequality in 1970. The actual Gini ratio was 363 in 1950 but the same relative budget would have yielded a post-fisc Gini of 383 in 1970. Either the tax system has grown less progressive over time and/or expenditures are less and less concentrated on low-income households than previously. Expansion in the relative size of the state is associated with smaller and smaller decrements in the Gini index, at least within the observed range.

TABLE 6.2

Gini Concentration Ratios for Post-Fisc Counterbudgets,
Standard Case, Factor Income

Year of NNP and Distributors	Year of Budget Share		
	1950	1961	1970
1950	363	330	313
1961	376	342	329
1970	383	353	339

A word of caution is in order here. The row comparisons of Gini coefficients are unambiguous in the sense that the Lorenz curves do not cross—the 1970 curve lies entirely within 1961, which, in turn, lies entirely within the 1950 curve. Increasing the share of NNP distributed by government, holding other factors constant, unambiguously shifts Lorenz curves toward the line of equality, and smaller Gini coefficients accurately portray these reductions. The comparisons of Gini ratios down the columns of table 6.2 are not unambiguous, however, because Lorenz curves intersect within each column. Holding the budget share constant and permitting changes in the initial distribution and the tax-expenditure distributors produce results which are difficult to interpret because Lorenz curves cross. Although the columns of table 6.2 shows slightly lower Gini ratios for the 1961 counter-budgets relative to those for 1970, the Lorenz curves are virtually indistinguishable and involve multiple intersections for each budget year. The 1950 budgets produce lower Gini ratios than both 1961 and 1970 and show a systematic departure in their Lorenz curves relative to those for 1961 and 1970. The 1950 Lorenz curves show higher cumulative shares of post-fisc income until approximately the 65th percentile, then a smaller share between the 65th and 90th percentiles, and approximately equivalent shares in the top 10 percent for all three years.

It may be helpful to summarize the evidence to this point. Over the period 1950–1970 the ratio of government taxes to NNP rose from 22 to 34 percent (a gain of 12 percentage points which is about the increase between 1902 and 1950) yet the post-fisc Gini coefficients fell by only 7 percent. The differences among post-fisc Gini ratios are not statistically significant. One reason post-fisc inequality failed to decline is that the pre-fisc Gini ratio for factor income increased by about 2 percent between 1961 and 1970. Between 1950 and 1961 the post-fisc Gini fell 6 percent. Almost all of the small decline in the estimated post-fisc Gini occurred during this eleven-year period when the distribution of factor earnings was stable. Note from table 5.1, however, that Gini coefficients are little different in all three years (384, 378, and 375 in 1950, 1961, and 1970 respectively) if general expenditures are distributed in a neutral way; the 6–7 percent decrease after 1950 falls to only 2 percent when general expenditures are not assumed to be redistributive toward lower incomes.

Several factors which affected the course of the post-fisc Gini coefficient from 1950 to 1970 have been identified in this and the preceding two chapters. Among these are:

1. The estimated Gini coefficient for factor income rose from 436 in both 1950 and 1961 to 446 in 1970. Most of the decline in the final Gini ratio occurred during the first decade when the initial concentration ratio was

stable. An interpretation is that the factors making for greater equality in the final income distribution just offset increasing inequality in factor incomes during the second decade, but such an interpretation assumes that the pre-fisc distribution is determined independently of government behavior.

2. The ratio of government taxes and expenditures to NNP rose throughout the period and was a persistent factor promoting greater equality in the post-fisc relative to the initial distribution. The relative growth of government was especially important during the period 1950– 1961, the same period in which post-fisc inequality experiences the bulk of its decline.

3. The assumption that one-half of the benefits of general expenditures accrue equally to all households is critical to the interpretation that growing government contributed to the decline in the post-fisc Gini ratio. If all the benefits of general expenditures are assumed to be neutrally distributed, even the small decline observed in the post-fisc Gini coefficient all but disappears.

4. The factors offsetting the expected decline in post-fisc inequality which would ordinarily accompany the relative growth of government, even if the growth were not in general expenditures, must involve the changing composition of taxes, transfers, and expenditures or else declining progressivity in the distribution of the tax burden or the distribution of expenditure benefits.

Sources of Declines in Gini Coefficients

If all taxes and expenditures were distributed by the initial distribution of income, Gini coefficients would be identical for the initial and post-fisc distributions. If all taxes and expenditures but one were distributed by the initial distribution of income in each year, any difference between the initial and post-fisc distributions could be attributed to the effects of that single tax or expenditure. Of course, this would be true only in an arithmetic sense, as is true of our other calculations, because the direct and indirect economic effects of the tax or expenditure are not measured. Nonetheless, distributing all but one tax or expenditure category by initial income provides a way to disaggregate the sources of lower post-fisc Gini coefficients in an additive manner. The size of any changes in Gini coefficients measured in this way would depend upon the size of the tax or expenditure and the nature of the incidence assumptions.

Table 6.3 shows the results of disaggregating the difference between initial coefficients and their respective post-fisc coefficients under normal

TABLE 6.3

Sources of Absolute Declines in Inequality, Normal Incidence, 1950, 1961, 1970, Factor NNP

	Gini × 1000		
	1950	1961	1970
1. General government	20	36	36
2. Taxes	10	5	-8[a]
a. Personal income	15	15	8
b. Social Security	-4[a]	-2[a]	-6[a]
c. Corporation income	4	3	2
d. Property tax	-3[a]	-5[a]	-7[a]
e. Other[b]	-4[a]	-6[a]	-5[a]
3. Transfer payments	25	36	53
a. Social Security	8	20	34
b. Other[c]	16	17	20
4. Other specific expenditures	16	18	26
a. Federal[d]	13	7	9
b. State and local[e]	2	10	17
5. Total	73	95	106

[a] Negative sign indicates that the item raises rather than lowers the post-fisc Gini coefficient relative to initial inequality.
[b] Sales, excises and customs, estate and gift taxes.
[c] Public assistance, other welfare, unemployment compensation, and other transfers.
[d] Veterans' benefits; Net interest paid; agriculture; elementary, secondary, and other education; higher education; highways; labor; and housing and community development.
[e] Veterans' benefits, net interest paid, agriculture, elementary, secondary, and other education; higher education, highways, and labor.

incidence assumptions. Each line was calculated by distributing all taxes and expenditures according to the initial distribution of factor income except for the item in question. Thus the decline due to Social Security taxes was calculated by distributing "other transfers," "specific federal expenditures," "the personal income tax," and so forth, according to initial income, but the Social Security tax was distributed by its standard distributor. Some striking features emerge. First, every expenditure category lowers the post-fisc Gini coefficient but not all taxes have that effect. For example, row 1 indicates the decrease in the concentration ratios arithmetically attributable to general government expenditures (normal incidence assumptions). General expenditures account for 27 percent (20/73) of the difference between the initial and the post-fisc Gini coefficient in 1950, 38 percent in 1961, and 34 percent in 1970. The effect of the declining progressivity of the tax structure (normal incidence) is traced out in line 2. Although taxes at all levels of government reduced the Gini ratio by small amounts in 1950 and 1961, by 1970 the tax structure actually increased the Gini ratio by a small amount. The decline between 1950 and 1970 in the progressivity of the tax system (−18 Gini points) more than offsets the growth of general government (+16 Gini points). The direction of change was common to each tax because, according to the comparisons in table 6.3, the federal personal income tax became less progressive while other taxes became more regressive. One surprise is that the growing regressivity of other taxes appears as important as the declining progressivity of the personal income tax. The same secular decline in the redistributive impact of the tax structure occurs if alternative but consistent incidence assumptions are used.

The decrease in Gini coefficients due to transfer payments grows dramatically between 1950 and 1970, almost entirely due to the growth in Social Security expenditures. The threefold increase in the contribution of Social Security benefits to declining Gini coefficients is due largely to the more than fivefold increase in the ratio of benefits paid to NNP over the period, because Social Security payments became substantially less pro-poor over the period. The evidence for this assertion is in Appendix B which shows that the lowest 14 percent of households received 62 percent of Social Security expenditures in 1950 but that the lowest 18 percent of households received only 30 percent of Social Security by 1970. Decreases in post-fisc Gini ratios due to other specifically allocable expenditures show only a slight upward trend, with state–local impact growing and the federal effect declining slightly. A major factor influencing the growing effect of state–local purchases was the more than threefold increase in elementary education expenditures. Elementary education expenditures, however, were also more pro-poor in 1970 than in 1950, as comparisons of the educational distributors in Appendix B demonstrate. For example, the Gini ratio for the educational distributor (children under age 18, item 19 in tables B.1–B.3) decreased from .28 in 1950 to .16 in 1970, indicating a change toward greater equality. Finally, there does not seem to be a large trend in the total decrease in concentration ratios due to the fisc if general expenditures are treated as neutral. If general expenditures are believed to be redistributive toward lower incomes, however, there is a trend toward larger differences between initial and post-fisc Gini coefficients.

More on Taxes

Declining progressivity in the effective tax schedule for all taxes was one factor diminishing the equalizing effect of government activity. As indicated in chapters 4 and 5, total taxes were less progressive in 1961 than in 1950 and may have become regressive by 1970. The linear regression estimates of taxes on income indicate that proportionality was gradually approached over time. The constant elasticity estimates were about one in 1950 but were less by 1970. Finally, as will be shown, the Gini coefficients of total taxes also declined revealing a secular decrease in the progressivity of the tax structure.

We can further pursue the role of taxes by considering a decomposition of their distributive impact into two components: first, changes in the relative dependence upon each type of tax, and second, changes in the progressivity of each type of tax. Table 6.4 describes the composition of taxes for each year and also reports the Gini coefficient for the respective distributor used in the standard incidence case. The Gini index provides a rough guide to the degree of progressivity for each tax. A value of 0 means that the tax is distributed equally by households; as the index rises toward 1, more of the tax burden falls upon higher incomes.

The most important changes in the composition of taxes between 1950 and 1970 have been the decline in corporate income taxes from 20 to 12 percent and the rise of Social Security taxes from 8 to 19 percent. This decreases the progressivity of the tax structure; but notice that the Gini ratios for the distribution of consumption expenditures and for dividends, each a distributor for one-half of corporate income taxes, have also declined. Another noticeable change in table 6.4 is the declining progressivity of incidence in the personal income tax, as indicated by the declining Gini coefficient from .667 in 1950 to .518 in 1970. If a tax starts out as progressive in the sense that the Gini ratio is higher than the Gini for

TABLE 6.4

The Tax Structure in 1950, 1961, and 1970

	1950		1961		1970	
Tax	Tax Share	Gini Ratio of Distributor	Tax Share	Gini Ratio of Distributor	Tax Share	Gini Ratio of Distributor
1. Personal income	.31	.667	.31	.593	.33	.518
2. Estate and gift	.02	.950	.02	.960	.02	.965
3. Corporate income	.10	.327	.08	.309	.06	.338
	.10	.761	.08	.706	.06	.652
4. Sales, customs, and excise	.26	.341	.24	.320[a]	.23	.338
5. Social Security	.08	.230	.15	.384	.19	.350
6. Property	.07	.327	.06	.309	.06	.338
	.07	.344	.06	.285	.06	.203

[a] The actual Gini ratio rather than the weighted sum of Gini ratios of the host of distributions indicated in the notes to the Appendix D tables.

factor income, a lower Gini coefficient over time usually can be interpreted as unfavorable for the low- and/or middle-income groups, at least approximately, because it means that the rich pay a smaller share of taxes and lower incomes pay a larger share. However, some of the Gini ratios are higher in later years, for example, the Social Security tax, which is favorable for lower-income households. Thus, changes are not all in a single direction and the information in table 6.4 does not permit any summary statement about the changing effects in the tax structure.

The Gini ratios for total taxes, however, show a decrease from .486 in 1950 to .453 in 1961 and .422 by 1970. This means that total taxes were considerably more concentrated among higher incomes in 1950 than in 1970, at least according to the Gini ratios. In fact, a Gini coefficient of .422 for taxes was below that for factor income (.446) in 1970, although it remained higher than the Gini ratio for money income in 1970 (.400). This is consistent with the results of table 6.3 which showed that by 1970 the total tax system actually raised the Gini coefficient relative to dispersion in factor income.

Since the declining Gini ratio for personal income taxes appears to play an important role in the evaporation of redistributive impact in the tax

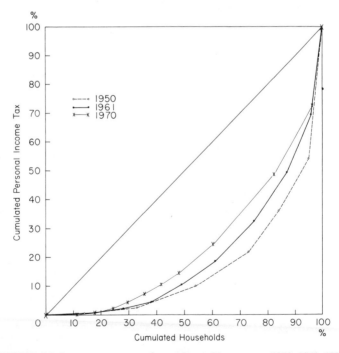

FIGURE 6.1 *Lorenz curve comparisons, personal income tax, 1950, 1961, 1970.*

system, figure 6.1 presents the Lorenz curves of personal income taxes for 1950, 1961, and 1970. The figure dramatically portrays the declining progressivity of the tax over the period. The shift of relative taxes paid away from the upper end toward the middle accounts for the declining concentration ratio for personal taxes, and the ineffectiveness of the personal income tax in reducing after-tax inequality.

Several factors might be cited to explain this pattern of declining concentration in the personal income tax. Probably the decision by state and local governments to fund an increasing share of their rapidly growing expenditures with the personal income tax diluted progressivity because their schedules are generally not as steeply graduated as the federal tax. Note that our data use the federal tax distributor for all personal income taxes collected, which means that this rationale cannot account for our numerical declines in concentration ratios. Another factor must involve growing nominal income and the nature of the changing schedule of rates. For example, the lowering of the upper limit to the federal tax rate, and the greater incentive to shelter income among a growing proportion of the population as their tax rates rose undoubtedly played a part, as did the increasing exemption limits at low-income levels.[1]

Another observation about the effect of the tax structure on post-fisc inequality is that the effect of growth in the Social Security tax is less than expected. The Social Security tax raises the post-tax Gini coefficient by only 4 points in 1950 and by 6 points in 1970. While the share of the Social Security tax in total federal taxes more than doubled over the twenty-year period, a substantial part of the increase came from higher taxable income limits which softened the potential regressive effects.

It is important to emphasize, once again, that all these allocations of the sources of the difference between the initial and the post-fisc distributions are arithmetic exercises only. They presume that the initial distribution was unaffected by expenditure and tax policies. Of course this is not generally the case, as we have argued in chapter 2. The assumptions which are used to calculate post-fisc income imply behavioral dependence of the initial income distribution upon the fisc. The assumption that a tax was shifted backward to factor owners implies that factor incomes of particular individuals would have been different without that tax. Whenever a tax was assumed to be shifted forward, it implies that the distribution of nominal

---

[1] M. Friedman provided some dramatic evidence about tax avoidance in a 1968 *Newsweek* column: "In the boom year 1929, more than 4,000 persons reported a taxable income of more than $250,000. Since then, our population has risen by more than 60 percent and average income has quadrupled—half real, half as a result of a doubling of prices. Hence, today's counterpart could be about 6,500 persons reporting a taxable income of more than $1 million. The actual number of million dollar taxable incomes reported in 1966 was 626" (reprinted in M. Friedman 1972, p. 76).

consumption differed from the distribution of real consumption due to the fisc. Hence, shifting taxes or expenditures could be responsible for the small increase in income inequality observed in the pre-fisc distribution.

Those analysts who prefer the concept of "broad income" as their income base are to some degree dealing explicitly with feedback from post-fisc to pre-fisc income implied by the presumption that taxes are shifted. For example, "broad income" would include the backward shifted portion of the various taxes.[2] The quantitative impact of this accounting procedure could be substantial. The Social Security tax raised the post-fisc Gini relative to the pre-fisc Gini by 6 points in 1970 but by only 2 Gini points in 1961. Since the Social Security tax is presumed to be entirely backward shifted, it would be consistent with the broad income concept to add the employers' portion of Social Security taxes paid to pre-fisc income, which would have lowered the Gini of pre-fisc income in 1970 relative to 1961. Since the employers' contribution is half the total Social Security tax, it accounted for roughly half the increase in the post-fisc Gini relative to the pre-fisc Gini over the decade, or about 2 Gini points. Over the period the pre-fisc Gini rose by 10 points, so that roughly 20 percent of that rise could be attributed, in an accounting sense, to the rise in the tax.

Other links between the fisc and the initial distribution of income have been frequently cited, though not always in the context of income distribution. The suspicion that higher levels of transfer payments are at least partly responsible for such demographic changes as the growing proportion of households headed by women, youth, and the aged is one example (Danziger and Plotnick 1975). Much of the talk about tax evasion, diminishing work incentives, and the declining after-tax return to risk taking also imply that the initial distribution is dependent upon the government budgets.

In Lieu of a Conclusion

Are there any presumptions that can be drawn from this chapter concerning the effects of the fisc on the distribution of income? Perhaps a conjecture is warranted. Figure 6.2 offers some possibilities from which to choose. This figure abstracts from possible long swings, from shorter business cycle fluctuations, and from the likelihood that pre-fisc inequality has probably always exceeded post-fisc inequality in this century, and presents some hypothetical scenarios for the course of income distributions in the twentieth century. The story represented in the first panel is that at some

---

[2] For a discussion of the analytical problems posed by the "broad income" concept, see chapter 2.

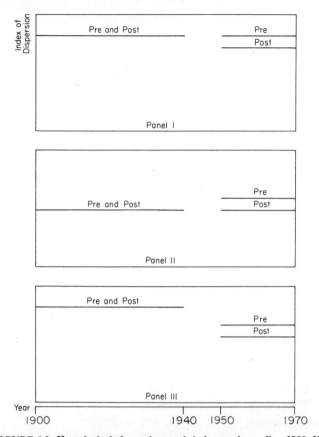

FIGURE 6.2 *Hypothetical alternative trends in income inequality, 1900-1970.*

time post-fisc dispersion dropped well below initial dispersion, with any feedback to pre-fisc inequality small enough to be ignored. The second panel presumes that post-fisc dispersion remained stable, and that the initial distribution entirely bore the distributive consequences of a relatively growing government. The third panel represents a common view among students of income dispersion. It posits a one time downward shift in both the pre- and post-fisc distributions, sometime during the 1930s or World War II, followed by stability. The slight upward trend in the pre-fisc distribution during the sixties may in part reflect the consequences of government budgets although the variation is probably well within the range of chance fluctuations which have occurred in the past.

Of course all this is conjecture. What we do know is that post-fisc inequality has been stable over the past twenty years and that it is arithmetically due to offsetting factors. The distributive effects of the fisc appear to be marked by a retreat from a progressive toward a neutral tax system, which has been offset by a rapid rise in cash transfers.

Postscript

Has the path of post-fisc inequality altered since 1970? A careful answer must be deferred until the results of the most recent Survey of Consumer Expenditures are available. However, recent changes in the relative size and composition of government payments and receipts can be previewed by a statistical experiment. Delayed publication of the complete set of National Income Account data for 1974 means that the most recent year for which this assessment can be made is 1973.

Not all the relevant trends in the composition of receipts and expenditures continued into 1973. Among those that did persist were the following: state and local tax receipts grew relative to federal tax receipts; the property tax declined in relative importance among sources of state and local revenues while the personal income tax continued to grow; the share of the Social Security tax in total federal taxes rose sharply (from 26 to 31 percent); and state and local expenditures increased more rapidly than federal expenditures and about as rapidly as state and local tax receipts. Among the trend reversals (all quite small, however) were: a fall in the share of the federal taxes coming from the personal income tax; an increase in the share of the corporate income tax and a decline in the share of general expenditures in federal expenditures; and a decline in the ratio of Social Security payments to NNP. Also, the ratio of government expenditures to NNP declined slightly and the ratio of taxes to NNP rose slightly. While these changes cut both ways, on balance it appears that they would generate a modest increase in the post-fisc Gini ratio between 1970 and 1973.

The statistical experiment does not support this interpretation. If the ratio of each category of expenditures and revenues to NNP in 1973 is assumed to hold in 1970 and the distribution of benefits and burdens of the standard 1970 case are also assumed to hold, the Gini coefficient for the resulting post-fisc distribution is .339. Post-fisc dispersion by this hypothetical standard is exactly what it was for the standard case in 1970.

7

An Assessment

In general, the art of government consists in taking as much money as possible from one class of citizens to give to the other. [Voltaire, *Dictionaire Philosophique*]

Summary of Major Findings

1. The size distribution of income is unconnected to any well-defined question of theory or policy, but there is widespread interest in it, probably for ideological reasons.

2. The fundamental question of ideological interest which is commonly pursued in studies of this kind cannot be answered empirically. We cannot know the behavioral effects of government upon the size distribution of income for three reasons:

(a) The effects of government which operate through channels other than the budget are pervasive.

(b) The counterfactual appropriate to evaluating the role of all government spending and taxation, a Lindahl equilibrium, cannot be empirically represented.

(c) Even particular programs, for example, the Old Age Survivors Disability and Health Insurance program, pose general equilibrium problems too complex to have been convincingly modeled thus far, much less produced implications confirmed by empirical tests.

3. A question which can be answered to a satisfactory degree of approximation is: What has been the course of income inequality over the postwar period when, after assigning the benefits of all public expenditures and the burden of all taxes, the value of Net National Product in a year is assigned to households?

4. After due celebration of the weaknesses of data and limitations of

method, it was nevertheless possible to draw the following conclusions with some confidence:

(a) Dispersion in the distribution of factor income increased slightly over the period. The difference was not statistically significant.

(b) Dispersion in the final distribution of income, which includes the benefits of government expenditures and the burdens of taxation, did not increase over the period and, if anything, decreased slightly. However, differences in final dispersion were generally not statistically significant.

(c) As a matter of simple arithmetic in which no account is taken of the behavioral responses of firms and households, it may be said that the net effect of government upon the final distribution is substantial in any year. That distribution of income which includes the benefits of government expenditures and the burdens of taxation is significantly closer to equality than the distribution of factor or money income in each year. However, the difference between the initial and final distributions arithmetically attributable to government in each year has not grown significantly over two decades despite the rapid growth in government. That is, the distributive impact of each dollar spent by government or taxed by government has declined, but the overall distributive effect remained at least as large because government spent and taxed on a much larger scale.

(d) Disaggregation revealed that the overall tax system had drifted from progressive to proportional or perhaps even to slightly regressive by 1970. The rapid rise in government transfer payments, especially Social Security, as well as other government spending, however, preserved or slightly increased the difference between initial and final distributions.

Some Caveats

We have not tried to conceal the empirical difficulties which have plagued our work. Some of the major problems bear repeating. First, the numerous comparisons between pre- and post-fisc distributions are subject to the conceptual reservations of chapter 2. That chapter illustrated how difficult it is to define a sensible pre-fisc distribution of income because the pre-fisc distribution is formed, in part, as a consequence of government behavior. Our preferred comparisons are not between distributions "without government" and "with government," but rather intertemporal comparisons among distributions which include government in each of them. The pre–post comparisons can only be interpreted as being of an accounting sort because they do not allow for direct and indirect behavioral responses to changes in government parameters. The quality of the data is the second

TABLE 7.1

Pechman–Minarik and Reynolds–Smolensky Compared, 1970

| | | Gini × 1000 | |
| | | Reynolds–Smolensky | |
Income Concept	Pechman–Minarik	Table 5.2	Reconciled
1. Money income	404	400	392
2. After taxes 1	389	NA	NA
3. After taxes 2	384	NA	384

NOTE: NA indicates "not available."

major problem area. In studies like this one, the accuracy and reliability of measurement is perhaps more troublesome than usual. The data for the distributors demanded by incidence theory are extensive, which often forces reliance upon multiple sources. Furthermore, some of the data are derived from household surveys, with all of the attendant pitfalls. An important aspect of this problem is whether the definitions of income which underlie the various distributors are similar enough for the purposes at hand. An objective standard by which disagreements on this issue could be resolved is lacking. We simply do not know. In deciding the host of empirical issues, we tended to opt for relative simplicity and for consistency across the years.

One test of the credibility of our results, admittedly weak, is to compare them with those of other researchers. While no other time series exists, we can compare our 1970 findings with those of Pechman and Minarik[1] for the same year. The results, which appear in table 7.1, are reassuring.

The Pechman–Minarik (P–M) data file is on an income base whose initial concentration ratio is closer to money income than to our factor income and hence in row 1 we compare their Gini coefficient with our money income base measure from chapter 5. Even though the P–M data are aggregated from individual household data and are corrected for underreporting, the two concentration ratios are quite similar. To some extent, however, the difference is too small because P–M included indirect business taxes in money income.[2] If indirect taxes are added to our money income base (column 3, row 1) the difference increases but only slightly.

---

[1] We are grateful to Pechman for suggesting the comparison and to Minarik for his patient provision of the data and supporting explanations which are from a manuscript in preparation. A fairly complete description of the P–M data base is in Pechman and Okner (1974). One difference is that the data for 1970 include the customs tax.

[2] Indirect business taxes were distributed by consumption and cash transfers by money income.

The Pechman–Minarik data base is designed to measure the effect of taxes on inequality, not the entire direct impact of the fisc, which limits the range of feasible comparisons. Making use of their microdata base, P–M assign taxes to recipient units and rerank them on their after-tax incomes. The Gini coefficient for P–M after-tax incomes is .389.[3] We cannot rerank, and our comparable concentration ratio is .384. The difference is small, and we apparently slightly underestimate the progressivity of the tax system since our gap between money income and posttax inequality is a bit smaller than theirs. If the P–M data is used with our reranking, their after-tax concentration ratio is identical to ours. Of course, this fortuitous outcome masks many differences in detail. We would conclude, however, that our approach, which is much cruder than that of Pechman and Minarik, is nevertheless adequate to the task at hand.

Thinking about the Results

Despite the differences in detailed procedures which distinguish the studies by different scholars, for each year studied similar results seem to recur time and again: the overall tax system is roughly proportional over most of the income range within which most households fall, and low-income households receive a relatively large share of expenditure benefits. The overall impact of government, then, appears to reduce the magnitude of income differences. If this is a real feature of the economy rather than just an accounting result out of the studies by Adler (1951), Conrad (1954), Pechman and Okner (1974), Musgrave et al. (1951), Gillespie (1965), Reynolds and Smolensky (1974), and so forth, it is eminently reasonable to ask why this pattern recurs so persistently. Nobody knows the answer but there are a number of hypotheses concerning why government redistributes income in the way that it does. The problem is to choose among them. The models are not well specified or are not rich enough in testable predictions to have permitted any hypothesis to yet emerge as the best single explanation.

James Rodgers (1974) has surveyed the models formulated to explain government redistribution and it is worthwhile to consider his review here. Rodgers suggests three general classes of models: narrow self-interest, insurance, and interdependent preferences. The first group of models, due particularly to Downs (1957), posits a democratic structure in which voters

[3] The P–M data were grouped into eleven income classes like those in the Reynolds–Smolensky calculations so that measurement error in the concentration ratios would be of similar magnitude. Using a maximum number of intervals raises the P–M Gini coefficient to .397.

form coalitions to use the state to confer benefits on coalition members and to disperse costs generally or to voters not in the coalition. In the simplest version of this model, voters are motivated by income alone and political parties compete for votes by promising to redistribute from those with high to those with low incomes. If a simple majority is required to gain or remain in office, the bottom 51 percent of the income distribution is a winning coalition, since it permits a larger amount of redistribution than a coalition of the top 51 percent.

A number of qualifications immediately arise. The coalition may not be stable because the richest one percent may be able to bribe some, especially the poorest, out of the majority coalition. Even the simplest version would not predict equalization of post-fisc incomes because impairment of effort of those in the top half would reduce the total available for redistribution. Many members of the majority coalition also have a positive probability of upward mobility in the income distribution which reduces the "Robin Hood" tendency. An important weakness of these models is the presumption that income is the sole criterion for political redistributive alliances. Characteristics like being a farmer, or in the maritime industry, or old, or a military veteran, or an automobile owner, or a college student often have more to do with success in gaining government benefits than current income. Self-interest models now fail to offer clear predictions about the patterns of redistribution by size class in democracies because of such qualifications. In any event, it is hard to believe that pure greed can explain everything. For example, low voter participation rates among the lowest income classes reduces the political benefits of redistributing income to them.

Another class of models is based upon the presumption that individuals are risk averse and prefer more stable incomes through time. Private arrangements supposedly fail to achieve an optimal set of arrangements for smoothing income flows which government then supplies through appropriate redistribution, e.g., social insurance schemes. Hence, although there is vertical redistribution at any point in time to those with temporarily low incomes, the present value expectations for each voter is zero lifetime redistribution. Presumably, unanimous consent to such an insurance scheme would require placing persons in different risk classes, with lower charges for higher income people. We would also expect eligibility for benefits to be based upon factors beyond low current income so as to reduce "moral hazard" problems. For example, various means tests for benefit eligibility would be used to reduce the cost of insurance and restrict payments to those who are poor due to causes largely beyond their control. Unfortunately, this kind of model is not well enough specified to test the validity of its predictions.

A final class of models relies upon the charitable motives of voters to explain redistribution by government. Presumably the income level or consumption rates of particular goods by some individuals enter as arguments in the utility functions of other individuals. If these charitable concerns cannot be fully or efficiently exploited through private transactions, government can "deftly" transfer income from the donors to the intended recipients (at small cost) and make both parties better off.

These political models may be promising but they are too rudimentary and indefinite to explain our results. They are addressed to the pattern of annual redistribution, a concept that, we have repeatedly emphasized, is not theoretically well specified, much less empirically investigated. These explanations have not proceeded far in answering their own implied question. They are also inadequate explanations for why the post-fisc distribution of income has shown no detectable overall change from 1950 to 1970.

Average income rose remarkably between 1950 and 1970, the government share has grown relative to the private sector, the composition of expenditures and taxes has changed, and yet on balance there is no detectable shift in the relative size of after-government income differences. Perhaps this phenomenon reflects some underlying behavioral regularity, but perhaps not. Simon Kuznets (Bronfrenbrenner 1971, p. 82) argued forcefully in another context that, ". . . the stability of many . . . economic statistics, if and when observed, is due to the balancing of conflicting effects of the underlying determinants; and its occurrence and continuity depend upon the occurrence and continuity of that balancing." As a matter of arithmetic this will always appear to be the case. We wonder, however. If the balancing of factors we observed in this study were not present, would another set of balanced forces have been observed? It appears to be a common view that, even in a predominantly market economy, the distribution of income, however defined, is subject to governmental manipulation. We are not convinced that the conventional wisdom is correct.

APPENDIX **A**

Algebraic Comparison of the
Definitions of Income Redistribution

The differences and similarities among the alternative definitions of redistribution can be clarified by presenting the components of each in algebraic form. Let P_i be the income earned by individual i in the primary distribution. Similarly, let F_i be the ith individual's final income. The effect of government redistribution on individual i is the difference between his final and primary income: $R_i \equiv F_i - P_i$ for $i = 1, \ldots, N$, where N is the number of individuals in the economy. Each definition of redistribution can be described by equations which identify the elements of R, in other words, the components and levels of income included in P for each definition of redistribution.

Income components

Y = pretax factor income
B = benefits of general government expenditures (i.e., expenditures other than transfers)
TD = nonrecipient benefits of transfers ("donor" benefits)
TRE = recipient benefits from efficient transfers
TRO = recipient benefits of transfers other than efficient transfers
TR = recipient benefits from all transfers, the sum of TRE and TRO
XM = taxes on a marginal benefit basis for benefits of general government expenditures and nonrecipient benefits from transfers
XA = taxes on an ability-to-pay basis
X = taxes paid, the sum of XM and XA

Benefits of general government expenditures (B) and nonrecipient benefits of transfers (TD) are valued at their marginal value to each individual. The benefits to recipients of in-kind transfers (a portion of TRE, TRO, and TR) are valued at their marginal values *net* of any charges to the recipient for goods and services included in these transfers. Recipient charges, therefore, are excluded from the tax components. This method of valuing recipient benefits of in-kind transfers allows us to exclude the marginal benefit taxes for these benefits from XM, which is necessary to obtain the simplified definitions at the bottom of table A.1.

Subscripts on income components denote the assumptions about governmental parameters under which the value of each component is determined. The subscripts for the four alternative assumptions relevant to the definitions of redistribution are:

n = government does not exist (i.e., taxes and government expenditures equal zero);
m = government exists, makes efficient allocative expenditures, and taxes according to marginal benefits received;
a = government exists, makes allocative expenditures and carries out redistributive policies according to an ability-to-pay principle to achieve an optimal distribution;
f = government exists, and pursues actual policies.

For example, Y_n denotes the factor income an individual would receive in long-run equilibrium with zero government, given existing technology, individual resource endowments, and individual preference functions.

To derive the components of R for each concept of redistribution, note first that the definition of final income is the same for all of the redistributive concepts under consideration. Events turn out in only one way each period. But this does not mean that the realized values of each component of income are the same for all individuals under all government policies; it only means that the components of income always sum up to total income. In our notation, final income is given by line 1 of table A.1. Final income, then, consists of factor payments plus all benefits of government expenditures (including recipient and nonrecipient benefits of all transfers) less taxes paid. All components of final income have an f subscript because they represent the actual values of the components in the time period in which redistribution is

TABLE A.1

Final Income, Primary Income, and Redistribution Specified

Final income (F)

(1) For all definitions of redistribution $\qquad Y_r + TR_r + TD_r + B_r - X_r$

Primary income (P)

(2) Case I $\qquad Y_n$

(3) Case II $\qquad Y_m + TRE_m + TD_m + B_m - XM_m$

(4) Case III $\qquad Y_m + TD_m + B_m - XM_m$

(5) Case IV $\qquad Y_a + TR_a + TD_a + B_a - (XM_a + XA_a)$

Redistribution (R)

(6) Case I $\qquad (Y_r - Y_n) + TR_r + TD_r + B_r - X_r$

(7) Case II $\qquad (Y_r - Y_m) + TRO_r + (TRE_r - TRE_m) + (TD_r - TD_m) + (B_r - B_m) - (X_r - XM_m)$

(8) Case III $\qquad (Y_r - Y_m) + TR_r + (TD_r - TD_m) + (B_r - B_m) - (X_r - XM_m)$

(9) Case IV $\qquad (Y_r - Y_a) + (TR_r - TR_a) + (TD_r - TD_a) + (B_r - B_a) - [X_r - (XM_a + XA_a)]$

Primary income (P) when XM = B + TD

(2') Case I $\qquad Y_n$

(3') Case II $\qquad Y_m + TRE_m$

(4') Case III $\qquad Y_m$

(5') Case IV $\qquad Y_a + TR_a - XA_a$

Redistribution (R) when XM = B + TD

(6') Case I $\qquad (Y_r - Y_n) + TR_r + TD_r + B_r - X_r$

(7') Case II $\qquad (Y_r - Y_m) + TRO_r + (TRE_r - TRE_m) + TD_r + B_r - X_r$

(8') Case III $\qquad (Y_r - Y_m) + TR_r + TD_r + B_r - X_r$

(9') Case IV $\qquad (Y_r - Y_a) + (TR_r - TR_a) + TD_r + B_r - (X_r - XA_a)$

measured. Of course, this does not imply that any data accurately report the appropriate values of these components.

The components and values of primary incomes vary with alternative concepts of redistribution, and are indicated in lines 2–5 of table A.1. In the zero government case, primary income is simply the factor income an individual would receive if there were no government, as indicated in line 2. By definition, benefits from government expenditures and the burdens of taxation are zero.

Under case II, primary income is given by line 3. Primary income in this case consists of factor payments under an efficient government plus all benefits of allocative activities of government including both recipient and nonrecipient benefits of efficient transfers minus marginal benefit taxes. The m subscript indicates that the values of all components are the equilibrium values which would prevail if the government engaged only in efficient amounts of allocative activity and taxed according to marginal benefits.

The definition of primary income for case III excludes recipient benefits from efficient transfers conducted by government, which is the only difference from the Case II definition. Recipient benefits from transfers are counted as part of redistribution under case III, and the expression for primary income is on line 4.

The case IV primary distribution is simply an expression for any primary, but it is assumed that the primary is an optimal distribution. It is constructed to maintain the rank order of individuals according to a counterfactual which defines equals and unequals, and is shown in line 5. Two kinds of taxation have been distinguished: ability-to-pay taxes are defined as deviations from marginal benefit taxes.

Subtracting each expression for primary income from final income yields expressions for the respective definitions of redistribution, which are shown in lines 6–9 of table A.1. These expressions can be simplified by noting that, by definition of marginal benefit taxation, $XM = B + TD$ for all i, that is, taxes paid equal the value of government benefits from general expenditures plus nonrecipient benefits from transfers under an efficient government. Therefore, these terms cancel, producing the simplified expressions at the bottom of table A.1, lines $2'$ to $9'$.

Of the four redistributive concepts, the simplest comparison is between case I and case III (lines 6 and 8). These differ only in the treatment of factor income. The similarity of the two definitions in other respects can best be explained by the definitions of primary income associated with these concepts. In going from the counterfactual of no government (n) to that of marginal benefit taxation (m) individuals have used income to "buy" collectively consumed goods. The benefits of these goods to any individual have been offset by taxes (since recipient benefits of efficient transfers are excluded from primary income in case III). The only change in any individual's income which occurs by the shift in counterfactuals is a change in his factor income due to the new allocation of resources. Therefore, only the exclusion of this effect of government from redistribution in case III distinguishes it from case I. Individual factor incomes change under the two variants because the demand for inputs shifts in the reallocation toward the production of collective goods. Supply schedules for factors, in turn, can shift because of these direct income effects as well as the income effect of the consumption of positive amounts of collective goods.

In contrast to case III, the case II concept (line 7) excludes *all* effects of allocative activities of government from redistribution. Case II excludes recipient benefits of efficient transfers as well as the change in factor income induced by allocative expenditures. The expressions for redistribution in table A.1 show the different treatment of transfers in cases II and III. All recipient benefits of transfers not justified on efficiency grounds are included in both variants. However, the only recipient benefits of efficient transfers included in case II result from a possible change in demand for efficient transfers induced by other redistributive policies.

Case IV redistribution is just the difference between the final distribution and the optimal distribution. It consists of (1) the differences between the factor income which individuals currently receive and that which they would receive under the optimal distribution (the first term), (2) differences between transfers received under the final and optimal distributions (the second term), and (3) the remaining deviations of current taxes from current benefits received after removing the deviations which would exist under the optimal distribution (the last three terms).

The expressions in table A.1 indicate the imposing data requirements and analytical problems involved in measuring redistribution by any of the definitions. In no case can the redistributive effects of government be calculated by looking at either the tax or expenditure side alone. All definitions require a determination of the difference in factor incomes between the final distribution and the counterfactuals. There is no reason to expect that these differences will be negligible. In addition, the case IV concept requires both a determination of individual incomes under a counterfactual which defines equals and unequals and an explicit choice of an ability-to-pay criterion. Finally, in case III, the level and distribution of efficient transfers under the m counterfactual must be determined. As Mishan (1972, pp. 973–74) has written, "In a community consisting of some scores of millions of adults, knowledge of the requisite pattern of interdependence is for all practical purposes unattainable. . . . Nothing less than detailed information about each person will ensure the consent of everyone involved."

Distributors by Income Class

TABLE B.1

Distributors by Income Class, 1950

Income Class	$0–$1000	$1000–$2000	$2000–$3000	$3000–$4000	$4000–$5000	$5000–$7500	$7500+	Total	Gini Ratio[a]
1. Households	14.0	19.0	21.0	19.0	11.0	11.0	5.0	100.0	NA
2. Money income	2.0	9.0	16.0	19.0	15.0	19.0	20.0	100.0	.391
3. Factor income	1.6	8.3	14.8	17.5	14.0	18.3	25.5	100.0	.437
4. Wages and salaries	1.4	8.2	14.5	17.2	14.0	18.5	26.3	100.1	.447
5. Dividends	2.0	3.0	4.0	5.0	4.0	10.0	72.0	100.0	.761
6. Interest income	6.0	9.0	15.0	15.0	11.0	18.0	26.0	100.0	.374
7. Rental income	1.4	8.2	14.5	17.2	14.0	18.5	26.3	100.1	.447
8. Net farm income	5.0	11.1	15.3	11.6	10.1	22.9	24.0	100.0	.376
9. Social Security benefits	61.6	12.8	9.9	6.5	4.3	4.6	0.3	100.0	—
10. Veterans' benefits	8.3	15.9	30.3	29.5	9.5	4.4	2.1	100.0	—
11. Public assistance	56.4	38.4	5.0	0.3	0.0	0.0	0.0	100.1	—
12. Personal income tax	0.5	2.0	7.5	12.0	14.0	18.0	46.0	100.0	.667
13. Estate and gift tax	0.0	0.0	0.0	0.0	0.0	0.0	100.0	100.0	.950
14. Social Security tax	2.4	10.4	24.5	26.1	15.4	13.9	7.3	100.0	.230
15. Estimated consumption	4.0	9.5	17.6	20.4	14.5	16.5	17.5	100.0	.327
16. Housing expenditures	2.8	9.5	17.9	21.3	13.9	14.9	19.7	100.0	.344
17. Auto expenditures	3.4	6.0	12.1	20.1	16.5	18.8	23.1	100.0	.440
18. Estimated expenditure on higher education	0.9	1.4	6.4	15.2	19.3	28.8	28.0	100.0	.621
19. Children under age 18	9.0	10.4	14.3	14.7	17.7	20.8	13.1	100.0	.278
20. Families in low-rent projects	11.7	43.6	30.5	9.4	4.8	0.0	0.0	100.0	—
21. Real property holdings	3.0	6.5	7.7	9.1	6.8	15.3	51.6	100.0	.604
22. Sales and gross receipts	3.2	9.2	17.5	21.3	14.4	16.4	18.0	100.0	.341
23. Covered wages	1.4	11.0	28.6	29.4	15.9	12.3	1.3	99.9	—

SOURCES: 1. Alfred H. Conrad, "Redistribution through government budgets in the United States, 1950," in Alan T. Peacock, ed., *Income redistribution and social policy* (London: Jonathan Cape, 1954), Chapter 6, Appendix table 1, pp. 226, 227, 266, and 267. Households are defined as Families and Unrelated Individuals.

2. *Ibid.*

3. Calculated from table C.1, lines 1–6.

4. Conrad, table 1, p. 197. Conrad's Original Income minus Transfers is used to distribute Wages and Salaries in constructing the Factor Income Base (see table C.1, line 1).

5. Same as line 1.

6. Same as line 1. The distributor is entitled Liquid Assets in Conrad.

7. Same as line 4. Original Income minus Transfers is used to distribute Rental Income in constructing the Factor Income Base (see table C.1, line 3).

8–9. Same as line 1.

10. Same as line 1. The distribution of Veterans is used as the distributor of Veterans' Benefits.

11. Same as line 1. The distribution of Families Receiving Aid for Dependent Children is used as the distributor of Public Assistance.

12. Conrad, table II A, pp. 204 and 266.

13–14. *Ibid.*

15. Same as line 1.

16. Conrad, Appendix table III, pp. 230 and 267. Housing Expenditures were calculated by summing the Housing Expenditures of Owners and Renters within an income class and dividing that sum by the sum of total Housing Expenditures of Owners and Renters.

17. *Ibid.*, Appendix table IV, pp. 231 and 267.

18. U.S. Bureau of the Census, with the cooperation of the Social Science Research Council, U.S. Department of Commerce, *Historical statistics of the United States: colonial times to 1957*, Series G 353–426 (Washington, D.C.: U.S. Government Printing Office, 1960), pp. G 353–408.

19. Calculated from Herman P. Miller, *Trends in the income of families and persons in the United States: 1947 to 1960*, Bureau of the Census Technical Paper No. 8, U.S. Department of Commerce (Washington, D.C.: U.S. Government Printing Office, 1963), table 5-1950, p. 126.

20–21. Same as line 1.

22. Same as line 12.

23. Same as line 1.

NOTE: All amounts are expressed as percentages. NA indicates "not applicable."

^a Gini ratios are not reported for cumulative distributions whose Lorenz curves lie entirely above the 45° line or intersect the 45° line.

TABLE B.2

Distributors by Income Class, 1961

Income Class	$0–$2000	$2000–$3000	$3000–$4000	$4000–$5000	$5000–$6000	$6000–$7500	$7500–$10,000	$10,000–$15,000	$15,000+	Total	Gini Ratio[a]
1. Households	18.0	10.0	10.0	11.0	12.0	14.0	12.0	9.0	4.0	100.0	NA
2. Money income	4.0	4.0	6.0	8.0	11.0	15.0	17.0	18.0	17.0	100.0	.398
3. Factor income	2.2	3.1	5.2	8.1	11.3	16.2	18.1	19.2	16.5	99.9	.436
4. Wages and salaries	1.3	2.6	4.9	8.8	12.4	18.2	20.2	19.9	11.7	100.0	.428
5. Dividends	0.8	1.7	4.6	2.7	5.0	5.4	6.9	19.8	53.1	100.0	.706
6. Interest income	5.4	8.0	7.7	6.9	6.9	9.3	12.7	16.3	26.8	100.0	.389
7. Rental income	14.0	8.2	6.9	6.4	5.8	7.9	11.1	12.4	27.3	100.0	.277
8. Net farm income	6.6	7.4	9.5	9.2	11.2	12.6	12.4	13.4	17.7	100.0	.276
9. Social Security benefits	27.0	18.2	15.0	8.5	8.7	8.7	6.8	5.9	1.2	100.0	—
10. Veterans' benefits	11.5	10.5	13.8	10.2	10.6	14.7	11.5	10.9	6.2	99.9	.075
11. Public assistance	57.8	20.7	6.4	4.2	4.4	2.4	1.5	2.6	0.0	100.0	—
12. Personal income tax	0.8	1.3	2.7	5.7	8.2	13.5	17.0	20.2	30.6	100.0	.593
13. Estate and gift tax	0.0	0.0	0.0	0.0	0.0	0.0	0.0	0.0	100.0	100.0	.960
14. Social Security tax	1.0	2.8	5.5	10.3	14.0	19.7	20.2	19.3	7.2	100.0	.384
15. Estimated consumption	5.7	5.2	6.8	9.3	12.0	16.4	17.2	16.5	10.9	100.0	.309
16. Housing expenditures	7.0	5.6	7.1	9.0	12.0	16.1	16.4	15.5	11.3	100.0	.285
17. Auto expenditures	2.4	4.0	7.1	10.5	13.6	19.0	18.3	16.8	8.2	99.9	.336
18. Estimated expenditure on higher education	1.6	1.7	2.6	5.0	8.2	12.5	15.7	27.3	25.4	100.0	.583
19. Children under age 18	6.5	7.5	9.1	12.9	15.2	18.9	15.5	10.4	3.9	99.9	.163
20. Excise and customs tax	3.9	4.3	7.0	9.7	12.4	17.3	18.1	17.6	9.6	99.9	.335
21. Other excise and sales tax	4.1	4.9	7.3	10.1	12.8	17.5	18.0	16.5	8.8	100.0	.311

SOURCES: 1. George Katona, Charles A. Lininger, and Richard F. Kosobud, *1962 Survey of Consumer Finances*, Monograph No. 32, Survey Research Center, Institute for Social Research (Ann Arbor, Mich: Univ. of Michigan, 1963), table 1-1, p. 10. Households are defined as Families and Unrelated Individuals. This line has not been adjusted since it is reported by pretax income intervals.

2. *Ibid.* This line has not been adjusted since it is reported by pretax income intervals.

3. Calculated from table C.2, lines 1–6.

4. Tax Foundation, Inc., *Tax burdens and benefits of government expenditures by income class, 1961 and 1965* (New York: Tax Foundation, 1967), table B-8, p. 47.

5–6. *Ibid.*

7. U.S. Department of the Treasury, Internal Revenue Service, *Statistics of income, 1961; individual income tax returns for 1961*, table 3, p. 36, Rents, Net Income in Adjusted Gross Income. This line has not been adjusted since it is reported by pretax income intervals.

8–9. Same as line 4.

10. Same as line 4. This is reported as Military Allotments and Pensions but is used by the Tax Foundation as the distributor for Veterans' Benefits.

11–16. Same as line 4.

17. Same as line 4. This distributor is listed as Auto Operation.

18–19. Same as line 4.

20. Same as line 4. This distributor is a combination of federal taxes on Alcoholic Beverages; Tobacco; Auto Purchase; and Telephone and Telegraph. It has been calculated by summing the dollar expenditures within an income class and dividing the sum by the total dollar expenditures on these items.

21. Same as line 4. This distributor is a combination of state and local taxes on Alcoholic Beverages, Tobacco, and Auto Purchase. It has been calculated by summing the dollar expenditures within an income class and dividing the sum by the total dollar expenditures on those items.

NOTE: All numbers are expressed as percentages. NA indicates "not applicable." All lines except 1, 2, and 7 have been adjusted by use of the procedure described on pp. 40–41 of the text.

[a] Gini ratios not reported for cumulative distributions whose Lorenz curves lie entirely above the 45° line or intersect the 45° line.

TABLE B.3

Distributors by Income Class, 1970

Income Class	$0–$2000	$2000–$3000	$3000–$4000	$4000–$5000	$5000–$6000	$6000–$7000	$7000–$8000	$8000–$10,000	$10,000–$15,000	$15,000–$25,000	$25,000+	Total	Gini Ratio[a]
1. Households	11.3	6.6	6.2	5.8	6.0	6.0	6.1	12.1	22.1	14.2	3.7	100.1	NA
2. Money income	1.3	1.7	2.2	2.7	3.4	4.0	4.7	11.2	27.8	27.2	13.7	99.9	.400
3. Factor income	0.8	1.3	1.8	2.4	3.1	3.7	4.5	10.7	26.8	26.9	17.9	99.9	.446
4. Wages and salaries	0.2	0.7	1.3	2.0	2.9	3.8	4.7	11.6	29.7	29.2	13.8	99.9	.452
5. Dividends	1.7	1.9	2.0	1.9	2.5	1.9	2.2	4.1	9.2	15.1	57.4	99.9	.652
6. Interest income	4.4	5.1	5.2	6.1	4.9	4.1	4.8	8.1	17.0	17.6	22.7	100.0	.272
7. Rental income	5.7	5.6	4.8	4.6	5.1	4.1	5.0	6.8	13.6	17.0	27.9	100.2	.293
8. Net farm income	4.6	4.3	5.5	6.1	6.2	6.5	6.5	10.9	20.4	17.0	12.0	100.0	.171
9. Social Security benefits	15.3	14.5	12.6	10.8	8.2	6.1	4.9	7.8	11.3	6.5	2.0	100.0	—
10. Veterans' benefits	5.4	8.5	8.6	6.9	6.2	6.1	4.7	10.3	22.9	16.7	3.7	100.0	.043
11. Public assistance	22.2	21.3	16.1	13.1	6.9	4.5	2.6	5.6	6.0	1.6	0.3	100.2	—
12. Personal income tax	0.1	0.7	1.4	2.2	2.8	3.4	4.0	9.7	24.5	23.7	27.4	99.9	.518
13. Estate and gift tax	0.0	0.0	0.0	0.0	0.0	0.0	0.0	0.0	0.0	0.0	100.0	100.0	.965
14. Social Security tax	0.9	1.3	2.4	3.1	4.1	4.8	5.9	13.8	29.0	24.0	10.8	100.1	.350
15. Estimated consumption	2.2	2.5	3.0	3.5	4.0	4.5	5.0	11.6	26.2	24.9	12.8	100.2	.338
16. Housing expenditures	6.1	4.5	4.3	4.2	5.0	4.7	5.0	11.4	24.6	21.7	8.6	100.1	.203
17. Auto expenditures	3.9	3.5	3.8	4.6	4.3	5.2	6.2	12.8	28.0	21.4	6.3	100.0	.223
18. Estimated expenditure on higher education	0.3	0.4	0.6	1.2	1.8	2.1	2.5	6.7	29.4	30.0	25.0	100.0	.579
19. Children under age 18	4.7	3.6	4.2	4.8	5.6	5.8	6.7	14.9	28.4	17.2	4.2	100.1	.155
20. Unemployment compensation	1.6	3.2	6.9	6.8	9.3	7.4	8.4	15.9	27.1	12.3	1.1	100.0	—
21. Other public transfers	1.7	5.2	3.6	4.3	6.0	5.7	5.7	11.9	26.6	22.3	7.0	100.0	.234
22. Estate and gift income	2.4	2.3	2.4	3.3	2.9	2.6	3.9	3.9	11.5	16.8	48.0	100.0	.561

SOURCES: 1. Dorothy S. Projector and Judith S. Bretz, "Measurement of transfer income in the Current Population Survey" (Paper delivered at the Conference on Research in Income and Wealth, the National Bureau of Economic Research, Pennsylvania State University, October 3–4, 1972), table 1, p. 30. Households are defined as Families and Unrelated Individuals. Partially published by same title in James D. Smith, ed., *The personal distribution of income and wealth* (New York: Columbia University Press, 1975), pp. 377–447.

2. *Ibid.*, table 5, p. 38.

3. Calculated from table C.3, lines 1–6.

4. Same as line 2.

5. U.S. Department of the Treasury, Internal Revenue Service, *Statistics of income 1970: individual income tax returns*, Preliminary (Washington, D.C.: U.S. Government Printing Office, 1972), table 4, p. 30, Dividends in Adjusted Gross Income.

6. *Ibid.*, p. 30, Interest Received.

7. *Ibid.*, p. 31, Rents, Net Income.

8. *Ibid.*, p. 29, Farm Income, Net Profit.

9. Projector and Bretz, table 7, p. 43.

10–11. *Ibid.*

12. U.S. Department of the Treasury, table 1, p. 22, Total Income Tax.

13. Distributed entirely to the highest income class. See tables B.1 and B.2.

14. Benjamin A. Okner, "Individual taxes and the distribution of income" (Paper prepared for the Conference on Research in Income and Wealth of the National Bureau of Economic Research, Pennsylvania State University, October 3, 1972). The Social Security Tax distributor assumes that both the employee and the employer components are borne entirely by the employee. It was estimated by using the effective tax rates as a percentage of 1966 income.

15. Tax Foundation, *Tax burdens and benefits of government expenditures by income class, 1961 and 1965* (New York: Tax Foundation, 1967). Consumption was estimated by assuming that the marginal propensity to spend from money income was the same in 1970 as in 1961. Estimate derived prior to rescaling 1961 income intervals.

16. Institute for Social Research, *A panel study of income dynamics: 1971 interviewing year, wave IV* (Ann Arbor, Mich.: University of Michigan, 1972), variables no. 23 and 426. The mean house value, by income class, as reported by the Michigan study, multiplied by the number of households, by income class, as reported by CPS, 1971 data. The distribution of the estimated House Value is used in the same manner as Housing Expenditures for 1950 and 1961.

17. *Ibid.*, variables no. 157 and 426. The mean number of Automobiles, by income class, as reported by the Michigan study, multiplied by the number of households, by income class, as reported by CPS, 1971 data. The distribution of Automobiles Owned is used in the same manner as Automobile Expenditures for 1950 and 1961.

18. Same as line 15. Expenditures on Higher Education were estimated by assuming that the marginal propensity to spend on higher education from money income, by income class, was the same in 1970 as in 1961. The resulting percentage distribution of dollar amounts appears to conform well to other studies of higher education, such as W. Lee Hansen and Burton A. Weisbrod, *Benefits, costs, and finance of public higher education* (Chicago: Markham Publishing, 1969).

19. U.S. Bureau of the Census, "U.S. Current Population Survey, 1971: employment histories of individuals in the labor force." Data obtained from the Center for Demography, University of Wisconsin, Madison, Family Records, Children 0–13, years; Person Records, Children 14–17 years.

20. Projector and Bretz, table 7, p. 43.

21. *Ibid.*

22. U.S. Department of the Treasury, table 4, p. 31, Estates and Trusts, Net Income.

NOTE: All amounts are expressed as percentages. NA indicates "not applicable."

ᵃ Gini ratio not reported for cumulative distributions where Lorenz curves lie entirely above the 45° line or intersect the 45° line.

APPENDIX C

Household Income Bases

TABLE C.1
Household Income Bases, 1950

Income Class	$0– $1000	$1000– $2000	$2000– $3000	$3000 $4000	$4000– $5000	$5000– $7500	$7500+	Total ($)[a]
1. Compensation of employees	2161	12,655	22,377	26,544	21,605	28,550	40,587	154,325
2. Proprietors income	506	2963	5240	6216	5060	6686	9505	36,140
3. Net rental income	119	695	1229	1457	1186	1568	2228	8473
4. Net interest	83	485	857	1017	828	1094	1555	5912
5. Corporate profits	491	2879	5090	6038	4915	6495	9233	35,106
6. Indirect business taxes	984	2337	4329	5017	3566	4058	4304	24,595
7. Total factor NNP	4343	22,013	39,122	46,290	37,160	48,450	67,413	264,551
8. Factor NNP per HH	597	2228	3583	4685	6497	8470	25,928	5088
9. Money NNP per HH	727	2410	3876	5088	6938	8788	20,350	5088
10. Percentage distribution factor NNP	1.6	8.3	14.8	17.5	14.0	18.3	25.5	100.0
11. Percentage distribution money NNP	2.0	9.0	16.0	19.0	15.0	19.0	20.0	100.0

SOURCES: 1. Table B.1, line 4, Wages and Salaries.

2–5. *Ibid.*

6. Table B.1, line 15, Estimated Consumption.

7. Calculated from lines 1–6.

8. Line 7 divided by table B.1, line 1, Households multiplied by the total number of households in 1950 (52 million).

9. Total NNP ($264,551 million) multiplied by table B.1, line 2, Money Income, divided by households in each income class as calculated in line 8 above.

10. Calculated from line 7.

11. Table B.1, line 2, Money Income.

NOTE: In dollars or millions of dollars.

[a] A. H. Conrad, "Redistribution through government budgets in the United States, 1950," in *Income redistribution and social policy,* ed. A. T. Peacock (London: Jonathan Cape, 1954), Appendix table 1, pp. 226, 227, 266, and 267. Households are defined as families and unrelated individuals.

TABLE C.2

Household Income Bases, 1961

Income Class	$0–$2000	$2000–$3000	$3000–$4000	$4000–$5000	$5000–$6000	$6000–$7500	$7500–$10,000	$10,000–$15,000	$15,000+	Total ($)[a]
1. Compensation of employees	3929	7858	14,810	26,598	37,479	55,009	61,054	60,147	35,363	302,246
2. Proprietors income	627	1254	2363	4243	5979	8776	9740	9596	5642	48,220
3. Net rental income	1712	1003	844	783	709	966	1358	1517	3339	12,231
4. Net interest	1085	1608	1548	1387	1387	1869	2553	3276	5387	20,100
5. Corporate profits	353	750	2030	1192	2207	2383	3045	8739	23,436	44,135
6. Indirect business taxes	2691	2455	3210	4390	5665	7742	8120	7789	5146	47,208
7. Total factor NNP	10,398	14,928	24,805	38,593	53,426	76,746	85,870	91,064	78,312	474,140
8. Factor NNP per HH	1044	2699	4485	6344	8050	9912	12,938	18,295	35,399	8573
9. Money NNP per HH	1908	3434	5152	6244	7871	9199	12,164	17,172	36,491	8586
10. Percentage distribution factor NNP	2.2	3.1	5.2	8.1	11.3	16.2	18.1	19.2	16.5	99.9
11. Percentage distribution money NNP	4.0	4.0	6.0	8.0	11.0	15.0	17.0	18.0	17.0	100.0

SOURCES: 1. Table B.2, line 4, Wages and Salaries.
2. *Ibid.*
3. *Ibid.*, line 7, Rental Income.
4. *Ibid.*, line 6, Interest Income.
5. *Ibid.*, line 5, Dividends.
6. *Ibid.*, line 15, Estimated Consumption.
7. Calculated from lines 1–6.
8. Line 7 divided by table B.2, line 1, Households multiplied by the total number of households in 1961 (55,307,000).
9. Total NNP ($474,865 million) multiplied by table B.2, line 2, Money Income, divided by households in each income class as calculated in line 8 above.
10. Calculated from line 7.
11. Table B.2, line 2, Money Income.

NOTE: In dollars or millions of dollars.

[a] Tax Foundation, *Tax burdens and benefits of government expenditures by income class, 1961 and 1965* (New York: Tax Foundation, 1967), Appendix table B-8, p. 47.

TABLE C.3

Household Income Bases, 1970

Income Class	$0–$2000	$2000–$3000	$3000–$4000	$4000–$5000	$5000–$6000	$6000–$7000	$7000–$8000	$8000–$10,000	$10,000–$15,000	$15,000–$25,000	$25,000+	Total ($)[a]
1. Compensation of employees	1204	4213	7824	12,037	17,454	22,871	28,287	69,816	178,752	175,743	83,056	601,858
2. Proprietors income	134	468	869	1337	1939	2541	3143	7757	19,860	19,526	9228	66,869
3. Net rental income	1329	1305	1119	1072	1189	956	1166	1585	3170	3963	6504	23,312
4. Net interest	1453	1684	1717	2014	1618	1353	1585	2674	5612	5810	7494	33,012
5. Corporate profits	1204	1346	1417	1346	1771	1346	1558	2904	6517	10,696	40,664	70,836
6. Indirect business taxes	1994	2266	2720	3173	3626	4079	4533	10,516	23,752	22,573	11,604	90,655
7. Total factor NNP	7317	11,282	15,665	20,979	27,597	33,146	40,271	95,252	237,663	238,311	158,546	886,542
8. Factor NNP per HH	961	2537	3750	5369	6827	8200	9799	11,684	15,962	24,910	63,602	13,146
9. Money NNP per HH	1514	3389	4669	6126	7457	8773	10,139	12,180	16,553	25,206	48,724	13,146
10. Percentage distribution factor NNP	0.8	1.3	1.8	2.4	3.1	3.7	4.5	10.7	26.8	26.9	17.9	99.9
11. Percentage distribution money NNP	1.3	1.7	2.2	2.7	3.4	4.0	4.7	11.2	27.8	27.2	13.7	99.9

SOURCES: 1. Table B.1, line 4, Wages and Salaries. (Includes proprietor income.)

2. *Ibid.*

3. *Ibid.*, line 7, Rental Income.

4. *Ibid.*, line 6, Interest Income.

5. *Ibid.*, line 5, Dividends.

6. *Ibid.*, line 15, Estimated Consumption.

7. Calculated from lines 1–6.

8. Line 7 divided by table B.2, line 1, Households multiplied by the total number of households in 1970 (67,372,000).

9. Total NNP ($886,546 million) multiplied by table B.2, line 2, Money Income, divided by households in each income class as calculated in line 8 above.

10. Calculated from line 7.

11. Table B.2, line 2, Money Income.

NOTE: In dollars or millions of dollars.

[a] U.S. Office of Business Economics, "National income and product in 1970," *Survey of Current Business* 51 (July 1971): Table 1.10, p. 16, National Income by Type of Income.

APPENDIX D

Taxes by Income Class

Federal Taxes by Income Class, 1950

Income Class	$0– $1000	$1000– $2000	$2000– $3000	$3000– $4000	$4000– $5000	$5000– $7500	$7500+	Total ($)[a]
1. Personal income	86	342	1283	2054	2396	3080	7872	17,113
2. Estate and gift	0	0	0	0	0	0	730	730
3. Corporate income	326	678	1172	1378	1004	1438	4857	10,854
4. Excise and customs	256	735	1398	1701	1150	1310	1438	7987
5. Social Security	85	370	871	928	547	494	260	3555
6. Total	752	2125	4724	6061	5097	6323	15,156	40,239
7. Per household	103	215	433	613	891	1105	5829	774

SOURCES: 1. Table B.1, line 12, Personal Income Tax.
2. *Ibid.,* line 13, Estate and Gift Tax.
3. *Ibid.,* one-half line 5, Dividends; one-half line 15, Estimated Consumption.
4. *Ibid.,* line 22, Sales and Gross Receipts.
5. *Ibid.,* line 14, Social Security Tax.
6. Sum of lines 1 through 5.
7. Line 6 divided by table B.1, line 1, Households, multiplied by the total number of households in 1950 (52 million).
NOTE: In dollars or millions of dollars.
[a] A. H. Conrad, "Redistribution through government budgets in the United States, 1950," in *Income redistribution and social policy,* ed. A. T. Peacock (London: Jonathan Cape, 1954), p. 204.

TABLE D.2

Federal Taxes by Income Class, 1961

Income Class	$0–$2000	$2000–$3000	$3000–$4000	$4000–$5000	$5000–$6000	$6000–$7500	$7500–$10,000	$10,000–$15,000	$15,000+	Total ($)[a]
1. Personal income	341	555	1152	2432	3499	5760	7254	8619	13,056	42,668
2. Estate and gift	0	0	0	0	0	0	0	0	1814	1814
3. Corporate income	707	750	1240	1305	1849	2371	2621	3948	6960	21,751
4. Excises and customs	570	622	963	1340	1729	2393	2472	2370	1342	13,806
5. Social Security	157	441	867	1622	2206	3104	3183	3041	1134	15,756
6. Total	1775	2369	4222	6700	9283	13,628	15,529	17,977	24,308	95,795
7. Per household	178	428	763	1101	1399	1760	2340	3612	10,988	1732

SOURCES: 1. Table B.2, line 12, Personal Income Tax.
2. *Ibid.*, line 13, Estate and Gift Tax.
3. *Ibid.*, one-half line 5, Dividends; one-half line 15, Estimated Consumption.
4. *Ibid.*, Distributed 57.4% line 20, Excise and Customs Tax; 16.8% line 17, Auto Expenditures; and 25.8% line 15, Estimated Consumption. Federal excise taxes on alcoholic beverages, tobacco, telephone and telegraph, auto purchase, auto operation and other excises were reported separately in Tax Foundation, *Tax burdens and benefits of government expenditures by income class, 1961 and 1965* (New York: Tax Foundation, 1967).
5. *Ibid.*, line 14, Social Security Tax.
6. Sum of lines 1 through 5.
7. Line 6 divided by table B.2, line 1, Households, multiplied by the total number of households in 1961 (55,307,000).
NOTE: In dollars or millions of dollars.
[a] Tax Foundation, pp. 48–49.

TABLE D.3

Federal Taxes by Income Class, 1970

Income Class	$0–$2000	$2000–$3000	$3000–$4000	$4000–$5000	$5000–$6000	$6000–$7000	$7000–$8000	$8000–$10,000	$10,000–$15,000	$15,000–$25,000	$25,000+	Total ($)[a]
1. Personal income	88	618	1237	1944	2474	3004	3534	8569	21,644	20,937	24,206	88,343
2. Estate and gift	0	0	0	0	0	0	0	0	0	0	3726	3726
3. Corporate income	598	675	767	828	997	982	1105	2409	5431	6137	10,770	30,684
4. Excises and custom	401	456	547	638	730	821	912	2116	4779	4542	2335	18,239
5. Social Security	444	641	1184	1529	2022	2367	2910	6806	14,302	11,836	5326	49,317
6. Total	1532	2391	3735	4939	6222	7174	8460	19,899	46,156	43,452	46,363	190,309
7. Per household	201	538	894	1264	1775	2059	2441	3100	4542	4542	18,599	2825

SOURCES: 1. Table B.3, line 12, Personal Income Tax.
2. *Ibid.*, line 13, Estate and Gift Tax.
3. *Ibid.*, one-half line 5, Dividends; one-half line 15, Estimated Consumption.
4. *Ibid.*, line 15, Estimated Consumption.
5. *Ibid.*, line 14, Social Security Tax.
6. Sum of lines 1 through 5.
7. Line 6 divided by table B.3, line 1, Households, multiplied by the total number of households in 1970 (67,372,000).

NOTE: In dollars or millions of dollars.

[a] U.S. Office of Business Economics, *Survey of Current Business* 51 (July 1971), table 3.1, p. 30.

State and Local Taxes by Income Class, 1950

Income Class	$0–$1000	$1000–$2000	$2000–$3000	$3000–$4000	$4000–$5000	$5000–$7500	$7500+	Total ($)[a]
1. Personal income	4	16	59	95	110	142	362	788
2. Estate and gift	0	0	0	0	0	0	421	421
3. Corporate income	18	37	64	75	55	79	265	593
4. Sales and excise	216	620	1180	1436	971	1106	1213	6741
5. Social Security	25	107	253	269	159	143	75	1031
6. Property	250	700	1308	1536	1046	1157	1370	7367
7. Total	513	1480	2863	3411	2341	2626	3708	16,941
8. Per household	70	150	262	345	409	459	1426	326

SOURCES: 1. Table B.1, line 12, Personal Income Tax.
2. *Ibid.*, line 13, Estate and Gift Tax.
3. *Ibid.*, one-half line 5, Dividends; one-half line 15, Estimated Consumption.
4. *Ibid.*, line 22, Sales and Gross Receipts.
5. *Ibid.*, line 14, Social Security Tax.
6. *Ibid.*, one-half line 15, Estimated Consumption; one-half line 16, Housing Expenditures.
7. Sum of lines 1 through 6.
8. Line 7 divided by table B.1, line 1, Households, multiplied by the total number of households in 1950 (52 million).
NOTE: In dollars or millions of dollars.
[a] A. H. Conrad, "Redistribution through government budgets in the United States, 1950," in *Income redistribution and social policy,* ed. A. T. Peacock (London: Jonathan Cape, 1954), p. 204.

TABLE D.5

State and Local Taxes by Income Class, 1961

Income Class	$0–$2000	$2000–$3000	$3000–$4000	$4000–$5000	$5000–$6000	$6000–$7500	$7500–$10,000	$10,000–$15,000	$15,000+	Total ($)ᵃ
1. Personal income	21	34	71	151	217	357	450	535	810	2648
2. Estate and gift	0	0	0	0	0	0	0	0	489	489
3. Corporate income	44	47	77	81	115	147	163	246	433	1353
4. Sales and excise	974	1007	1437	2008	2589	3559	3640	3436	2071	20,726
5. Social Security	57	159	312	585	796	1120	1149	1097	410	5685
6. Property	1139	969	1247	1641	2153	2915	3014	2870	1991	17,938
7. Total	2236	2216	3144	4467	5871	8099	8414	8182	6204	48,839
8. Per household	225	401	568	734	885	1046	1268	1644	2804	883

SOURCES: 1. Table B.2, line 12, Personal Income Tax.
2. *Ibid.*, line 13, Estate and Gift Tax.
3. *Ibid.*, one-half line 5, Dividends; one-half line 15, Estimated Consumption.
4. *Ibid.*, distributed 11% table B.2, line 21, Other excise and sales tax; 25%, line 17, Auto Expenditures; 64%, line 15, Estimated Consumption, state and local sales and excise taxes on alcoholic beverages, tobacco, general sales, auto purchase, auto operation, and other excises were reported separately in Tax Foundation, *Tax burdens and benefits of government expenditures by income class, 1961 and 1965* (New York: Tax Foundation, 1967).
5. *Ibid.*, line 14, Social Security Tax.
6. *Ibid.*, one-half line 15, Estimated Consumption; one-half line 16, Housing Expenditures.
7. Sum of lines 1 through 6.
8. Line 7 divided by table B.2, line 1, Households, multiplied by the total number of households in 1961 (55,307,000).

NOTE: In dollars or millions of dollars.

ᵃ Tax Foundation, pp. 48–49.

TABLE D.6
State and Local Taxes by Income Class, 1970

Income Class	$0–$2000	$2000–$3000	$3000–$4000	$4000–$5000	$5000–$6000	$6000–$7000	$7000–$8000	$8000–$10,000	$10,000–$15,000	$15,000–$25,000	$25,000+	Total ($)[a]
1. Personal income	11	78	156	245	311	378	445	1078	2723	2634	3045	11,114
2. Estate and gift	0	0	0	0	0	0	0	0	0	0	1082	1082
3. Corporate income	68	77	87	94	114	112	126	275	619	700	1228	3499
4. Sales and excise	1093	1242	1491	1739	1988	2236	2484	5764	13,019	12,373	6360	49,690
5. Social Security	75	108	199	258	341	399	490	1147	2410	1994	897	8309
6. Property	1519	1281	1336	1410	1647	1684	1831	4210	9299	8530	3917	36,611
7. Total	2767	2786	3269	3745	4401	4809	5376	12,474	28,070	26,231	16,530	110,305
8. Per household	363	627	783	958	1089	1190	1308	1530	1885	2742	6631	1637

SOURCES: 1. Table B.3, line 12, Personal Income Tax.
2. *Ibid.*, line 13, Estate and Gift Tax.
3. *Ibid.*, one-half line 5, Dividends; one-half line 15, Estimated Consumption.
4. *Ibid.*, line 15, Estimated Consumption.
5. *Ibid.*, line 14, Social Security Tax.
6. *Ibid.*, one-half line 15, Estimated Consumption; one-half line 16, Housing Expenditures.
7. Sum of lines 1 through 6.
8. Line 7 divided by table B.3, line 1, Households, multiplied by the total number of households in 1970 (67,372,000).
NOTE: In dollars or millions of dollars.
[a] U.S. Office of Business Economics, *Survey of Current Business* 51 (July 1971), table 3.3, p. 26.

APPENDIX E

Expenditures by Income Class

TABLE E.1

Federal Expenditures by Income Class, 1950

Income Class	$0–$1000	$1000–$2000	$2000–$3000	$3000–$4000	$4000–$5000	$5000–$7500	$7500+	Total ($)[a]
1. National defense, international affairs and space research	1334	2335	3062	3122	2138	2506	2609	17,106
2. Other general expenditures	362	633	831	847	580	680	708	4641
3. Social Security	1363	283	219	144	95	102	7	2213
4. Veterans' benefits	550	1054	2008	1955	630	292	139	6627
5. Net interest paid	282	423	705	705	517	846	1222	4700
6. Agriculture	139	309	426	323	281	638	668	2784
7. Elementary, secondary, and other education	0	0	0	0	0	0	0	0
8. Higher education	1	2	7	17	22	33	32	114
9. Highways	0	0	0	0	0	0	0	0
10. Labor	4	22	38	45	37	49	69	263
11. Housing and community development	31	114	80	25	13	0	0	261
12. Total	4066	5174	7376	7183	4313	5144	5453	38,709
13. Per household	559	524	675	727	754	899	2097	744

SOURCES: 1. Table B.1, one-half line 1, Households; one-half line 3, Factor Income. These expenditures were referred to as Military Service and International Security in A. H. Conrad, "Redistribution through government budgets in the United States, 1950," in *Income redistribution and social policy*, ed. A. T. Peacock (London: Jonathan Cape, 1954).

2. *Ibid.* Expenditures include General Government; Transportation and Communication; Finance, Commerce, Industry; and Natural Resources, reported separately in Conrad.

3. *Ibid.*, line 9, Social Security Benefits.

4. *Ibid.*, line 10, Veterans' Benefits.

5. *Ibid.*, line 6, Interest Income.

6. *Ibid.*, line 8, Net Farm Income.

7. Not reported separately.

8. Same as line 1. Line 18, Estimated Expenditure on Higher Education. Referred to as Education and General Research in Conrad.

9. Not reported separately.

10. Same as line 1. Line 4, Wages and Salaries.

11. *Ibid.*, line 20, Families in Low-rent Projects. Included in General Government Expenditure in 1961 and 1970.

12. Sum of lines 1 through 11.

13. Line 12 divided by table B.1, line 1, Households, multiplied by the total number of households in 1950 (52 million).

NOTE: In dollars or millions of dollars.

a Conrad, table III A, pp. 214 and 66.

TABLE E.2

Federal Expenditures by Income Class, 1961

Income Class	$0–$2000	$2000–$3000	$3000–$4000	$4000–$5000	$5000–$6000	$6000–$7500	$7500–$10,000	$10,000–$15,000	$15,000+	Total ($)[a]
1. National defense, international security, and space research	5194	3368	3908	4911	5991	7765	7740	7251	5271	51,426
2. Other general expenditures	936	607	704	885	1080	1399	1395	1307	950	9268
3. Social Security	3766	2539	2092	1186	1213	1213	948	823	167	13,948
4. Veterans' benefits	706	645	848	627	651	903	706	670	381	6143
5. Net interest paid	344	509	490	439	439	592	808	1038	1706	6366
6. Agriculture	263	295	378	366	446	501	494	533	704	3980
7. Elementary, secondary, and other education	20	23	28	39	46	58	47	32	12	305
8. Higher education	3	4	5	11	17	26	33	58	54	211
9. Highways	111	126	190	271	350	485	486	456	261	2738
10. Labor	8	15	29	52	74	108	120	118	70	595
11. Public assistance and other welfare	1654	592	183	120	126	69	43	74	0	2862
12. Total	13,005	8723	8857	8907	10,434	13,120	12,821	12,359	9577	97,842
13. Per household	1306	1577	1601	1464	1572	1694	1932	2483	4329	1769

SOURCES: 1. Table B.2, one-half line 1, Households; one-half line 3, Factor Income.

2. *Ibid.* Expenditures include general government (excluding interest), transportation (excluding highways), commerce and finance, housing and community development, health and sanitation, civilian safety, and miscellaneous.

3. *Ibid.*, line 9, Social Security Benefits.

4. *Ibid.*, line 10, Veterans' Benefits.

5. *Ibid.*, line 6, Interest Income.

6. *Ibid.*, line 8, Net Farm Income.

7. *Ibid.*, line 19, Children under Age 18.

8. *Ibid.*, line 18, Estimated Expenditure on Higher Education.

9. *Ibid.*, one-half line 17, Auto Expenditures; one-half line 15, Estimated Consumption. Line 17, Auto Expenditures, was the only distributor used in 1950 and 1970. Estimated consumption is larger than auto expenditures in the two extreme classes.

10. *Ibid.*, line 4, Wages and Salaries.

11. *Ibid.*, line 11, Public Assistance. All Public Assistance appears as State and Local Government Expenditures in 1970.

12. Sum of lines 1 through 11.

13. Line 12 divided by table B.2, line 1, Households, multiplied by the total number of households in 1961 (55,307,000).

NOTE: In dollars or millions of dollars.

[a] Tax Foundation, *Tax burdens and benefits of government expenditures by income class, 1961 and 1965* (New York: Tax Foundation, 1967, table B-7, p. 45.

TABLE E.3

Federal Expenditures by Income Class, 1970

Income Class	$0–$2000	$2000–$3000	$3000–$4000	$4000–$5000	$5000–$6000	$6000–$7000	$7000–$8000	$8000–$10,000	$10,000–$15,000	$15,000–$25,000	$25,000+	Total ($)[a]
1. National defense, international affairs, and space research	5278	3446	3489	3577	3969	4231	4623	9944	21,328	17,926	9421	87,232
2. Other general expenditures	840	548	555	569	632	673	736	1583	3394	2853	1499	13,883
3. Social Security	6309	5979	5196	4453	3381	2515	2021	3216	4660	2680	825	41,235
4. Veterans' benefits	532	838	848	680	611	602	463	1016	2258	1647	365	9861
5. Net interest paid	647	749	764	896	720	603	705	1190	2498	2586	3336	14,696
6. Agriculture	212	198	254	281	286	300	300	502	940	784	553	4610
7. Elementary, secondary, and other education	57	44	51	58	68	70	81	181	345	209	51	1214
8. Higher education	1	1	2	4	6	7	8	23	99	101	84	336
9. Highways	8	7	7	9	8	10	12	25	54	41	12	193
10. Labor	1	3	6	10	14	19	23	57	146	144	68	493
11. Unemployment compensation	63	126	271	267	365	291	330	625	1065	483	43	3930
12. Other transfers	52	158	109	131	182	173	173	362	808	677	213	3038
13. Total	13,999	12,098	11,553	10,936	10,244	9493	9476	18,724	37,596	30,132	16,470	180,721
14. Per household	1839	2721	2766	2799	2534	2348	2306	2297	2525	3150	6607	2682

SOURCES: 1. Table B.3, one-half line 1, Households; one-half line 3, Factor Income.
2. *Ibid.* Expenditures include general government (excluding interest), transportation (excluding highways), commerce and finance, housing and community development, health and sanitation, civilian safety, and miscellaneous.
3. *Ibid.*, line 9, Social Security Benefits.
4. *Ibid.*, line 10, Veterans' Benefits.
5. *Ibid.*, line 6, Interest Income.
6. *Ibid.*, line 8, Net Farm Income.
7. *Ibid.*, line 19, Children under Age 18.
8. *Ibid.*, line 18, Estimated Expenditure on Higher Education.
9. *Ibid.*, line 17, Auto Expenditure.
10. *Ibid.*, line 4, Wages and Salaries.
11. *Ibid.*, line 20, Unemployment Compensation. Not reported separately in 1950 and 1961.
12. *Ibid.*, line 21, Other Public Transfers. Not reported separately in 1950 and 1961.
13. Sum of lines 1 through 12.
14. Line 13 divided by table B.3, line 1, Households, multiplied by the total number of households in 1970 (67,372,000).
NOTE: In dollars or millions of dollars.
a U.S. Office of Business Economics, *Survey of Current Business* 51 (July 1971), table 3.10, p. 36.

State and Local Expenditures by Income Class, 1950

Income Class	$0–$1000	$1000–$2000	$2000–$3000	$3000–$4000	$4000–$5000	$5000–$7500	$7500+	Total ($)[a]
1. General expenditures	254	445	584	595	408	478	497	3261
2. Public assistance	2203	1500	195	12	0	0	0	3906
3. Veterans' benefits	39	74	141	137	44	20	10	464
4. Net interest paid	26	38	64	64	47	76	110	425
5. Agriculture	4	9	13	10	8	19	20	83
6. Elementary secondary and other education	283	327	449	462	556	653	411	3141
7. Higher education	4	6	26	62	79	118	114	408
8. Highways	108	191	384	639	524	597	734	3177
9. Labor	0	0	0	0	0	0	0	0
10. Total	2920	2589	1856	1979	1666	1962	1897	14,865
11. Per household	401	262	170	200	291	343	730	286

SOURCES: 1. Table B.1, one-half 1, Households; one-half line 3, Factor Income. Expenditures include Natural Resources, Police and Fire Protection, Sanitation, and General Government and Miscellaneous, which were reported separately in A. H. Conrad, "Redistribution through government budgets in the United States, 1950," in *Income redistribution and social policy,* ed. A. T. Peacock (London, Jonathan Cape, 1954).
2. *Ibid.,* line 11, Public Assistance. Expenditures are Relief and General Welfare and Health and Hospitals, which were reported separately in Conrad.
3. *Ibid.,* line 10, Veterans' Benefits.
4. *Ibid.,* line 6, Interest Income.
5. *Ibid.,* line 8, Net Farm Income.
6. *Ibid.,* line 19, Children under Age 18.
7. *Ibid.,* line 18, Estimated Expenditure on Higher Education.
8. *Ibid.,* line 17, Auto Expenditures.
9. Not reported separately in Conrad.
10. Sum of lines 1 through 9.
11. Line 10 divided by table B.1, line 1, Households, multiplied by the total number of households in 1950 (52 million).
NOTE: In dollars or millions of dollars.
[a] Conrad, table III B, pp. 215 and 266.

TABLE E.5

State and Local Expenditures by Income Class, 1961

Income Class	$0–$2000	$2000–$3000	$3000–$4000	$4000–$5000	$5000–$6000	$6000–$7500	$7500–$10,000	$10,000–$15,000	$15,000+	Total ($)[a]
1. General expenditures	1787	1159	1345	1690	2062	2672	2663	2495	1814	17,696
2. Public assistance	2430	1232	779	454	467	422	322	308	51	6466
3. Veterans' benefits	13	12	16	12	12	17	13	12	7	113
4. Net interest paid	41	61	59	53	53	71	97	125	205	766
5. Agriculture	35	39	50	48	59	66	65	70	93	524
6. Elementary, secondary, and other education	1061	1224	1485	2105	2481	3085	2530	1697	637	16,321
7. Higher education	47	50	77	148	242	369	463	806	750	2951
8. Highways	255	289	437	623	805	1113	1116	1047	601	6289
9. Labor	0	0	0	1	1	2	2	2	1	10
10. Total	5669	4067	4248	5133	6181	7817	7272	6563	4158	51,136
11. Per household	569	735	768	844	931	1010	1096	1318	1880	925

SOURCES: 1. Table B.2, one-half line 1, Households; one-half line 3, Factor Income. Expenditures include general government (except interest), transportation (except highways), commerce and finance, housing and community development, health and sanitation, civilian safety, and miscellaneous.
2. *Ibid.*, distributed 34.4 percent line 1, Public Assistance, and 65.6 percent line 9, Social Security Benefits. Public assistance and social insurance benefits are combined here as Public Assistance but were reported separately in Tax Foundation, *Tax burdens and benefits of government expenditures by income class, 1961 and 1965* (New York: Tax Foundation, 1967).
3. *Ibid.*, line 10, Veterans' Benefits.
4. *Ibid.*, line 6, Interest Income.
5. *Ibid.*, line 8, Net Farm Income.
6. *Ibid.*, line 19, Children under Age 18.
7. *Ibid.*, line 18, Estimated Expenditure on Higher Education.
8. *Ibid.*, one-half line 17, Auto Expenditures; one-half line 15, Estimated Consumption.
9. *Ibid.*, line 4, Wages and Salaries.
10 Sum of lines 1 through 9.
11. Line 10 divided by table B.2, line 1, Households, multiplied by the total number of households in 1961 (55,307,000).
NOTE: In dollars or millions of dollars.
[a] Tax Foundation, table B-7, p. 45.

131

TABLE E.6

State and Local Expenditures by Income Class, 1970

Income Class	$0–$2000	$2000–$3000	$3000–$4000	$4000–$5000	$5000–$6000	$6000–$7000	$7000–$8000	$8000–$10,000	$10,000–$15,000	$15,000–$25,000	$25,000+	Total ($)[a]
1. General expenditures	2690	1756	1778	1823	2023	2156	2356	5069	10,871	9137	4802	44,462
2. Public assistance	3695	3546	2680	2181	1149	749	433	932	999	266	50	16,646
3. Veterans' benefits	0	0	0	0	0	0	0	0	0	0	0	0
4. Net interest paid	0	0	0	0	0	0	0	0	0	0	0	0
5. Agriculture	59	55	70	78	79	83	83	139	259	216	153	1272
6. Elementary, secondary, and other education	2018	1546	1803	2061	2404	2490	2877	6397	12,193	7385	1803	42,934
7. Higher education	34	45	68	136	204	238	283	759	3330	3397	2831	11,325
8. Highways	604	542	589	713	666	806	960	1983	4337	3315	976	15,491
9. Labor	2	6	11	17	25	33	41	101	259	254	120	871
10. Total	9102	7496	7000	7008	6550	6555	7033	15,379	32,248	23,971	10,735	133,001
11. Per household	1196	1686	1676	1793	1620	1622	1711	1887	2166	2506	4306	1974

SOURCES: 1. Table B.3, one-half line 1, Households; one-half line 3, Factor Income. Expenditures include general government (excluding interest), transportation (excluding highways), commerce and finance, housing and community development, health and sanitation, civilian safety, and miscellaneous.
2. Ibid., line 11, Public Assistance.
3. Included in Federal Expenditures.
4. Not reported separately in U.S. Office of Business Economics, Survey of Current Business 51 (July 1971), table 3.10, p. 30.
5. Same as line 1. Line 8, Net Farm Income.
6. Ibid., line 19, Children under Age 18.
7. Ibid., line 18, Estimated Expenditure on Higher Education.
8. Ibid., line 17, Auto Expenditures.
9. Ibid., line 4, Wages and Salaries.
10. Sum of lines 1 through 9.
11. Line 10 divided by table B.3, line 1, Households, multiplied by the total number of households in 1970 (67,372,000).
NOTE: In dollars or millions of dollars.
[a] U.S. Office of Business Economics.

References

Aaron, H., and McGuire, M. C. 1970. Public goods and income distribution. *Econometrica* 38:907–920.

Aaron, H.; Musgrave, R. A.; Brazer, H.; Netzer, D.; Friedlander, A.; Rolph, E.; and Peterson, G. 1974. The property tax: progressive or regressive. *American Economic Association Papers and Proceedings* 64:212–35.

Adelman, I.; and Morris, C. T. 1973. *Economic growth and social equity in developing countries.* Stanford, Calif.: Stanford Univ. Press.

Adler, J. H. 1951. The fiscal system, the distribution of income, and public welfare. In *Fiscal policies and the American economy,* ed. K. Poole, pp. 359–409. Englewood Cliffs, N.J.: Prentice-Hall.

Aitchison, J., and Brown, J. A. C. 1957. *The lognormal distribution.* London: Cambridge Univ. Press.

Arrow, K. 1951. *Social choice and individual values.* New York: John Wiley and Sons.

Atkinson, A. B. 1970. On the measure of inequality. *Journal of Economic Theory* 2:244–63.

Barna, T. 1945. *Redistribution of incomes through the fiscal system in 1937.* Oxford: Oxford Univ. Press.

Becker, G. S. 1973. A theory of marriage: part I. *Journal of Political Economy* 81:813–46.

———. 1974. A theory of marriage: part II. *Journal of Political Economy* 82:S11–S26.

Behrens, J., and Smolensky, E. 1973. Alternative definitions of income redistribution. *Public Finance/Finances Publiques* 28:315–32.

Ben Porath, Y. 1967. The production of human capital and the life-cycle of earnings. *Journal of Political Economy* 75:352–65.

Benham, F. C. 1934. Notes on the pure theory of public finance. *Economica* 1:436–58.

Benus, J., and Morgan, J. N. 1975. Time period, unit of analysis, and income concept in the analysis of income distribution. In *The personal distribution of income and wealth,* ed. J. D. Smith, pp. 209–24. National Bureau of Economic Research, Conference on Research in Income and Wealth. New York: Columbia Univ. Press.

Bishop, G. A. 1966. Income redistribution in the framework of the national income accounts. *National Tax Journal* 19:378–90.

Blinder, A. S. 1975. Distribution effects and the aggregate consumption function. *Journal of Political Economy* 83:447–75.

Boulding, K. E. 1975. The stability of inequality. *Review of Social Economy* 33:1–14.

Boulding, K. E., and Pfaff, M., eds. 1972. *Redistribution to the rich and the poor.* Belmont, Calif.: Wadsworth Publishing.

Brady, D. S. 1951. Research on the size distribution of income. In National Bureau of Economic Research, *Conference on research in income and wealth,* pp. 2–53. Studies in Income and Wealth, no. 13. New York: National Bureau of Economic Research.

———. 1965. *Age and the income distribution.* Washington, D.C.: U.S. Government Printing Office.

Bronfenbrenner, M. 1971. *Income distribution theory.* Chicago: Aldine–Atherton.

———. 1973. Equality and equity. *Annals of the American Academy of Political and Social Science* 409:81–91.

Brown, C. V. 1973. *The impact of tax changes on income distribution.* London: Institute for Fiscal Studies.

Browning, E. K. 1973. Social insurance and intergenerational transfers. *Journal of Law and Economics* 16:215–37.

Buchanan, J. M. 1970. *The public finances.* Homewood, Ill.: Richard D. Irwin.

Budd, E. C. 1970. Postwar changes in the size distribution of income in the U.S. *American Economic Review* 60:247–60.

Budd, E. C.; Radner, D. B.; and Hinrichs, J. C. 1973. *Size distribution of family personal income: methodology and estimates for 1964.* Bureau of Economic Analysis Staff Paper, no. 21. Washington, D.C.: U.S. Department of Commerce.

Champernowne, D. G. 1974. A comparison of measures of income distribution. *Economic Journal* 84:787–816.

———. 1953. A model of income distribution. *Economic Journal* 63:318–51.

Chiswick, B. 1974. *Income inequality.* New York: Columbia Univ. Press.

Chow, G. C. 1960. Tests of equality between sets of coefficients in two linear regressions. *Econometrica* 28:591–605.

Clark, C. 1937. *National income and outlay.* London: Macmillan.

Conrad, A. H. 1954. Redistribution through government budgets in the United States, 1950. In *Income redistribution and social policy,* ed. A. T. Peacock, pp. 178–267. London: Jonathan Cape.

Cooter, R., and Helpman, E. 1974. Optimal income taxation for transfer payments. *Quarterly Journal of Economics* 88:656–70.

Cragg, J. C.; Harberger, A. C.; and Mieszkowski, P. 1967. Empirical evidence on the incidence of the corporation income tax. *Journal of Political Economy* 75:811–21.

Cramer, J. S. 1969. *Empirical econometrics.* Amsterdam: North Holland.

Dalton, H. 1920. *Some aspects of inequality of incomes in modern communities.* London: G. Routledge and Sons. Quoted in D. S. Brady, Research on the size distribution of income. In *Conference on research in income and wealth,* pp. 2–53. Studies in Income and Wealth, no. 13. New York: National Bureau of Economic Research, 1951.

Danziger, S., and Plotnick, R. 1975. *Demographic change, government transfers, and the distribution of income.* Discussion Paper Series, no. 274. Madison: Institute for Research on Poverty, Univ. of Wisconsin.

Danziger, S., and Smolensky, E. 1975. *Income inequality: problems of measurement and interpretation.* Discussion Paper Series, no. 304. Madison: Institute for Research on Poverty, Univ. of Wisconsin.

Dasgupta, P.; Sen, A. K.; and Starret, D. 1973. Notes on the measurement of inequality. *Journal of Economic Theory* 6:180–87.

Davis, O. A.; Dempster, M. A. H.; and Wildavsky, A. 1966. A theory of the budgeting process. *American Political Science Review* 60:529–47.

———. 1966. On the process of budgeting: an empirical study of congressional appropriation. *Public Choice* 1:63–132.

Dodge, D. A. 1975. Impact of tax, transfer, and expenditure policies of government on the distribution of personal income in Canada. *Review of Income and Wealth,* series 21, no. 1, pp. 1–52.

Downs, A. 1957. *Economic theory of democracy.* New York: Harper and Row.

Eapen, A. T. 1966. Federalism and fiscal equity reconsidered. *National Tax Journal* 19:325–29.

Elteto, O., and Frigyes, E. 1968. New income inequality measures as efficient tools for causal analysis and planning. *Econometrica* 36:383–95.

Fair, R. C. 1971. The optimal distribution of income. *Quarterly Journal of Economics* 85:551–79.

Feldstein, M. 1974. Social Security, induced retirement, and aggregate capital accumulation. *Journal of Political Economy* 82:905–26.

Fishlow, A. 1972. Brazilian size distribution of income. *American Economic Review* 62:391–402.

Foley, D. K. 1970. Lindahl's solution and the core of an economy with public goods. *Econometrica* 38:66–72.

Friedman, M. 1953a. Choice, chance, and the personal distribution of income. *Journal of Political Economy* 4:277–90.

———. 1953b. *Essays in positive economics.* Chicago: Univ. of Chicago Press.

———. 1962. *Capitalism and freedom.* Chicago: Univ. of Chicago Press.

———. 1972. *An economist's protest.* Glen Ridge, N.J.: Thomas Horton.

Galbraith, J. K. 1958. *The affluent society.* Boston: Houghton Mifflin.

Gastwirth, J. L. 1972. The estimation of the Lorenz curve and Gini index. *Review of Economics and Statistics* 54:306–16.

Gibrat, R. 1931. *Les inegalités economiques.* Paris: Sirey.

Gillespie, W. I. 1965. Effect of public expenditures on the distribution of income. In *Essays in fiscal federalism,* ed. R. A. Musgrave, pp. 122–186. Washington, D.C.: Brookings Institution.

Goldsmith, S.; Jaszi, G.; Kaitz, H.; and Liebenberg, M. 1954. The size distribution of income since the mid-thirties. *Review of Economics and Statistics* 36:1–32.

Gordon, R. J. 1967. The incidence of the corporation income tax in manufacturing, 1925–62. *American Economic Review* 57:731–58.

Hansen, W. L., and Weisbrod, B. A. 1969. *Benefits, costs, and finance of public higher education.* Chicago: Markham.

Haveman, R. H. 1965. *Water resource investment and the public interest.* Nashville: Vanderbilt Univ. Press.

Henle, P. 1972. Exploring the distribution of earned income. *Monthly Labor Review* 95:16–27.

Hochman, H. M., and Rodgers, J. D. 1969. Pareto optimal redistribution. *American Economic Review* 59:542–57.

Institute for Social Research. 1972. *A panel study of income dynamics: 1971 interviewing year, wave IV.* Ann Arbor: Univ. of Michigan.

Johansen, L. 1968. *Public economics.* Chicago: Rand McNally.

Johnson, H. G. 1973. Some micro-economic reflections on income and wealth inequalities. *Annals of the American Academy of Political and Social Science* 409:53–60.

Kakwani, N. C., and Podder, N. 1973. On the estimation of Lorenz curves from grouped observations. *International Economic Review* 14:278–92.

Kondor, Y. 1971. An old–new measure of income inequality. *Econometrica* 39:1041–42.

Kravis, I. 1962. *The structure of income.* Philadelphia: Univ. of Pennsylvania Press.

Krzyzaniak, M., and Musgrave, R. A. 1963. *The shifting of the corporation income tax.* Baltimore: Johns Hopkins Press.

Kuznets, S. 1955. Economic growth and income inequality. *American Economic Review* 45:1–18.

Lampman, R. J. 1957. Recent thought on egalitarianism. *Quarterly Journal of Economics* 71:234–66.

———. 1969. Transfer and redistribution as social process. In *Social Security in international perspective,* ed. S. Jenkins, pp. 29–54. New York: Columbia Univ. Press.

———. 1973. Measured inequality of income: what does it mean and what can it tell us. *Annals of the American Academy of Political and Social Science* 409:81–91.

Lerner, A. P. 1944. *The economics of control.* New York: Macmillan.

Lindahl, E. 1958. Just taxation—a positive solution. In *Classics in the theory of public finance,* ed. R. A. Musgrave and A. T. Peacock, pp. 168–76. London: Macmillan.

Lydall, H. 1968. *The structure of earnings.* Oxford: Oxford Univ. Press, Clarendon Press.

Mandelbrot, B. 1962. Paretian distributions and income maximization. *Quarterly Journal of Economics* 76:57–85.

———. 1970. The Pareto–Levy law and the distribution of income. *International Economic Review* 1:79–106.

Marshall, A., ed. 1948. *Principles of economics.* 8th ed. New York: Macmillan.

McLure, C. E., Jr. 1974. On the theory and methodology of estimating benefit and expenditure incidence. Mimeographed. Houston: Rice Univ.

Meade, J. E. 1964. *Efficiency, equality, and the ownership of property.* Cambridge, Mass.: Harvard Univ. Press.

Meerman, J. P. 1974. The definition of income in studies of budget incidence and income distribution. *Review of Income and Wealth,* series 20, no. 4, pp. 515–22.

Mera, K. 1969. Experimental determination of relative marginal utilities. *Quarterly Journal of Economics* 83:464–77.

Metcalf, C. E. 1972. *An econometric model of the income distribution.* Chicago: Markham.

———. 1974. The size distribution of current income: the ′N–P′ distribution. Mimeographed. Madison: Univ. of Wisconsin.

Miller, H. 1963. Trends in the income of families and persons in the United States: 1947 to 1960. U.S. Department of Commerce, Bureau of Census Technical Paper, no. 8. Washington, D.C.: U.S. Government Printing Office.

Mincer, J. 1970. The distribution of labor incomes: a survey with special reference to the human capital approach. *Journal of Economic Literature* 8:1–26.

———. 1974. *Schooling, experience, and earnings.* New York: Columbia Univ. Press.

Mincer, J., and Chiswick, B. 1972. Time series changes in personal income inequality in the United States from 1939, with projections to 1985. *Journal of Political Economy* 80:534–66.

Mirlees, J. A. 1971. An exploration of the theory of optimal income taxation. *Review of Economic Studies* 38:175–208.

Mishan, E. J. 1972. The futility of Pareto-efficient distributions. *American Economic Review* 62:971–76.

Morgan, J. N.; David, M.; Cohen, W.; and Brazer, H. 1962. *Income and welfare in the United States.* New York: McGraw-Hill.

Morgenstern, O. 1963. *On the accuracy of economic observations.* Princeton, N.J.: Princeton Univ. Press.

Musgrave, R. A. 1959. *The theory of public finance.* New York: McGraw-Hill.

Musgrave, R. A.; Carroll, J. J.; Cook, L. D.; and Frane, L. 1951. Distribution of tax payments by income groups: a case study for 1948. *National Tax Journal* 4:1–53.

Musgrave, R. A., and Musgrave, P. G. 1973. *Public finance in theory and practice.* New York: McGraw-Hill.

Musgrave, R. A.; Case, K.; and Leonard, H. 1974. The distribution of fiscal burdens and benefits. *Public Finance Quarterly* 2:259–300.

National Bureau of Economic Research. 1951. *Conference on research in income and wealth.* Studies in Income and Wealth, no. 13. New York: National Bureau of Economic Research.

———. 1973. *53rd annual report.* New York: National Bureau of Economic Research.

Okner, B. A. 1972. Individual taxes and the distribution of income. Mimeographed. Washington, D.C.: Brookings Institution.

Paglin, M. 1975. The measurement and trend of inequality: a basic revision. *American Economic Review* 65:598–609.

Paukert, F. 1973. Income distribution at different levels of development: a survey of evidence. *International Labor Review* 108:97–125.

Pechman, J. A., and Okner, B. A. 1974. *Who bears the tax burden?* Washington, D.C.: Brookings Institution.

Pigou, A. C. 1928. *A study in public finance.* London: Macmillan.

Prest, A. R. 1955. Statistical calculations of tax burdens. *Economica* 22:234–45.

Projector, D. S., and Bretz, J. S. 1972. Measurement of transfer income in the Current Population Survey. Mimeographed. New York: National Bureau of Economic Research. Partially published in *The personal distribution of income and wealth,* ed. J. D. Smith, pp. 377–477. National Bureau of Economic Research, Conference on Research in Income and Wealth. Studies in Income and Wealth, no. 39. New York: Columbia Univ. Press, 1975.

Pryor, F. L. 1973. Simulation of the impact of social and economic institutions on the size distribution of income and wealth. *American Economic Review* 63:50–72.

Radner, D. B., and Hinrichs, J. C. 1974. Size distribution of income in 1964, 1970, and 1971. *Survey of Current Business* 54:19–31.

Rawls, J. 1971. *A theory of justice.* Cambridge, Mass.: Harvard Univ. Press, Belknap Press.

Reynolds, M., and Smolensky, E. 1974. The post fisc distribution: 1961 and 1970 compared. *National Tax Journal* 27:515–30.

Rivlin, A. M. 1975. Income distribution—can economists help? *American Economic Review* 65:1–15.

Rodgers, J. D. 1974. Explaining income distribution. In *Redistribution through public choice,* ed. H. M. Hochman and G. E. Peterson, pp. 165–205. New York: Columbia Univ. Press.

Rosten, L. 1968. *The joys of Yiddish.* New York: McGraw-Hill.

Rutherford, R. S. G. 1955. Income distributions: a new model. *Econometrica* 23:277–94.

Schnitzer, M. 1974. *Income distribution.* New York: Praeger.

Schultz, T. P. 1969. Secular trends and cyclical behavior of income distribution in the United States, 1944–1965. In *Six papers on the size distribution of wealth and income,* ed. L. Soltow, pp. 75–100. National Bureau of Economic Research, Conference on Research in Income and Wealth. Studies in Income and Wealth, no. 33. New York: Columbia Univ. Press.

———. 1972. Long term change in personal income distributions. *American Economic Review* 62:361–62.

Scitovsky, T. 1973. Inequalities: open and hidden, measured and immeasurable. *Annals of the American Academy of Political and Social Science* 409:112–19.

Sen, A. 1973. *On economic inequality.* New York: W. W. Norton.

Sheshinski, E. 1972. Relation between a social welfare function and the Gini index of inequality. *Journal of Economic Theory* 4:98–100.

Smith, A. 1950. *The wealth of nations.* London: Methuen.

Smith, J. D., ed. 1975. *The personal distribution of income and wealth.* National Bureau of Economic Research, Conference on Research in Income and Wealth. Studies in Income and Wealth, no. 39. New York: Columbia Univ. Press.

Soltow, L., ed. 1969. *Six papers on the size distribution of wealth and income.* National Bureau of Economic Research, Conference on Research in Income and Wealth. Studies in Income and Wealth, no. 33. New York: Columbia Univ. Press.

Stark, T. 1972. *The distribution of personal income in the United Kingdom.* London: Cambridge Univ. Press.

Stoikov, V. 1975. How misleading are income distributions? *Review of Income and Wealth,* series 21, no. 2, pp. 239–50.

Survey Research Center. 1961. *1960 survey of consumer finances.* Ann Arbor: Institute for Social Research, Univ. of Michigan.

———. 1963. *1962 survey of consumer finances.* By G. Katona; C. A. Lininger; and R. F. Kosobud. Ann Arbor: Institute for Social Research, Univ. of Michigan.

———. 1969. *1968 survey of consumer finances.* By G. Katona; W. Dunkelberg; J. Schmiedeskamp; and F. Stafford. Ann Arbor: Institute for Social Research, Univ. of Michigan.

———. 1973. *1971–72, surveys of consumers.* By L. Mandel; G. Katona; J. N. Morgan; and J. Schmiedeskamp. Ann Arbor: Institute for Social Research, Univ. of Michigan.

Tax Foundation. 1967. *Tax burdens and benefits of government expenditures by income class, 1961 and 1965.* New York: Tax Foundation.

Thiel, H. 1967. *Economics of information theory.* Amsterdam: North Holland.

Thompson, E. 1974. Taxation and national defense. *Journal of Political Economy* 82:755–82.

Thurow, L. C. 1971. The income distribution as a pure public good. *Quarterly Journal of Economics* 85:327–36.

Tinbergen, J. 1975. *Income distribution: analyses and policies.* Amsterdam: North Holland.

Tobin, J. 1970. On limiting the domain of inequality. *Journal of Law and Economics* 13:263–77.

U.S. Bureau of the Budget, Office of Statistical Standards. 1966. Family income distribution statistics. *American Statistician* 20:18–20.

U.S. Council of Economic Advisers. 1972. *Economic report of the president.* Washington, D.C.: U.S. Government Printing Office.

U.S. Department of Commerce, Bureau of the Census, with the cooperation of the Social Science Research Council. 1960. *Historical statistics of the United States: colonial times to 1957,* series G, pp. 353–426. Washington, D.C.: U.S. Government Printing Office.

U.S. Department of Commerce. 1966. *The national income and product accounts of the United States, 1929–1965: statistical tables.* Washington, D.C.: U.S. Government Printing Office.

U.S. Department of Labor, Bureau of Labor Statistics. 1971. *Consumer expenditure and income: survey guidelines.* Bulletin no. 1684. Washington, D.C.: U.S. Government Printing Office.

U.S. Department of the Treasury, Internal Revenue Service. 1964. *Statistics of income, 1961; individual income tax returns for 1961.* Washington, D.C.: U.S. Government Printing Office.

U.S. Department of the Treasury, Internal Revenue Service. 1972. *Statistics of income 1970: individual income tax returns.* Preliminary. Washington, D.C.: U.S. Government Printing Office.

U.S. Office of Business Economics. 1971. *Survey of Current Business,* vol. 51.

U.S. Office of Business Economics. 1973. *Survey of Current Business,* vol. 53.

Vanderbilt, A. 1963. *New complete book of etiquette.* Garden City, N.Y.: Doubleday.

Watts, H. W. 1967. The iso-prop index: an approach to the determination of poverty income thresholds. *Journal of Human Resources* 2:3–18.

———. 1968. An economic definition of poverty. In *On understanding poverty,* ed. D. P. Moynihan, pp. 316–29. New York: Basic Books.

———, and Peck, J. K. 1975. On the comparison of income redistribution plans. In *The personal distribution of income and wealth,* ed. J. D. Smith, pp. 75–118. National Bureau of Economic Research, Conference on Research in Income and Wealth. Studies in Income and Wealth, no. 39. New York: Columbia Univ. Press.

Weintraub, S., ed. 1973. Income inequality. *Annals of the American Academy of Political Science* 409:*viii–x.*

Weisbrod, B. A. 1968. Income redistribution effects and benefit cost analysis. In *Problems in public expenditure analysis,* ed. S. P. Chase, pp. 177–208. Washington, D.C.: Brookings Institution.

Wicksell, K. 1958. A new principle of just taxation. In *Classics in the theory of public finance,* ed. R. A. Musgrave and A. T. Peacock, pp. 72–118. London: Macmillan.

Wiles, P. 1974. *Distribution of income: east and west.* Amsterdam: North Holland.

Subject Index